JESUS!

His Birth, Death and Resurrection

A Revisionist Analysis of the
"Sacrosanct" Christian Viewpoint

Charles S. Brown

JESUS!

His Birth, Death and Resurrection

A Revisionist Analysis of the "Sacrosanct" Christian Viewpoint

Charles S. Brown.

http://www.crystalbooks.org

This Edition published in New Zealand by
Crystal Publishing
P.O. Box 60042, Titirangi,
West Auckland,
NEW ZEALAND.

First Edition 2005
Second Edition 2007

Final Edition 2012

Cover: **"The Transfiguration of Christ"** by Fra Angelico (ca. 1441 AD)

ISBN 978-0-9582813-8-6

Contents

Acknowledgements

Crystal Publishing gratefully and singularly acknowledges **Ferrar Fenton** – long deceased from the physical world – yet whose monumental work of re-translating **The Bible** finally permitted certain key questions in centuries-old conflicts between science and religion e.g., – Creation versus Evolution – to be perfectly reconciled. Through his intuitively-correct translation of **The Book of Genesis**, particularly Chapters 1 and 2, he has singularly rendered *every other* "Genesis" translation – that does not accord with his powerfully-guided, correct insights – irrelevant. Near-future events will unequivocally bear out the truth of this statement.

His crucial spiritual insights have therein returned to **THE CREATOR** that which is **HIS**: –
The Majesty and Power of The Pure Truth of His stupendous and humanly-incomprehensible Creation.

Fenton has therewith bequeathed to the worlds of science and religion the ordained foundation upon which to build, within their Disciplines:

The 'Harmonising Truth' about Creation and Evolution; and thus the True Origins of Man!

Fenton's correct translation of **The Book of Genesis** therefore permits certain questions about the **Life, Death and Resurrection of Jesus** to be answered more logically than is possible with other Bibles. More especially on the key aspect of Jesus's birth, since **The Son Of God Himself** – in order for a time to be a "man among men" – had also to be born of a woman of earth.

Precisely *because* the ***Creation/Evolution*** reality deriving from **Immutable Divine Law** has been *correctly understood* by

5

Fenton, the logical extrapolation from such sure insight also logically means that *his* translation and insights thus offer greater enlightenment than do other mainstream Bibles.

So among the very many Bible translations inundating global Christendom therefore; **Ferrar Fenton's Bible** stands as the strongest overall.

Introduction

For the roughly two billion Christians who comprise "global Christendom", a revisionist analysis of key and sacrosanct tenets of 'the Faith' might be seen as a possible blasphemous challenge to the very cornerstone of the Christian "reason for being". That being the case, coupled with the fact that thousands of books have been written about Jesus by all manner of learned and "unlearned" writers both from within and without Christendom, where might I fit in this "many-writers" group?

In the present, academic achievements and intellectual sophistry are lauded virtually above all else. These two 'cornerstones' of world and 'worldly' education hold powerful sway in probably most Universities, and thus strongly drive the 'learning paradigm' in many countries. Anyone writing 'theologically', as it were, is invariably expected to have at least some 'University letters' after their name. On that basis with regard to this Booklet and the subject matter it examines, one *could* therefore *perhaps* dismiss it without any examination whatsoever for, *on the surface*, it evidences not even a hint of *academic* qualifications *for the author*.

However, in the many and *seemingly* irreconcilable points of disputation even between various Christian denominations and their ***individualised Bibles***; in *this* case on the subject matter herein, *this* Booklet provides ***especial*** and ***decisive*** insights that cut completely across long-held and appalling distortions about the life and death of The Son Of God; primarily from the leaders and "Bible scholars" of mainstream Christendom. And we elucidate it all without the need for 'letters' and/or 'educational titles'.

Despite the very large numbers of well-educated and 'many-lettered' Bible-authors who continually *theorise* on the life and meaning of Jesus's tenure on earth, the "on-the-ground reality" of differing views about Him in global societies, in the end translates to tension; either overt or covert. And at times, even conflict.

With regard to *my* 'qualifications', therefore: In Truth, I possess no academic refinement from any worldly "Institution of Higher Learning". However, what I do have *in the first instance* is simple 'common sense' coupled with a logical-thinking mind. For the particular subject that this Booklet examines, the 'logical-thinking' aspect is perhaps brutally so. But, therewith, precisely the *'right stuff'* to strip away the strongly-promoted yet often conflicting notions of Christendom on the very especial life of Jesus, to *thereby reveal* a very different and far more logical view of His time as "a man among men".

In the pages of **this** Booklet; you, the reader, **will discover this clear fact for yourself.**

So, do I possess *any* mandate at all? Yes, I most certainly do! But not from a University or similar. For this work, I accept the mandate given by Paul, The Apostle of **Jesus; The Son of God!**

From Paul, founder of "The Church": For University academics, for Christian theologians and for the reader of this book; I accept as *my* clear mandate the directive *he* gave to *his* followers.

Originally stated in **Preface** and **Epilogue** in the Parent Work, the subject matter of this Booklet – which necessarily uses The Bible as its primary source – calls for it to also be aired here; *before* we *seriously begin* our contentious analyses.

Accepted as a noted *intellectual thinker and scholar* by Christian academics throughout history and by *many of the same today*, let us all take note of Paul's clear admonition to the academic elite of *his* time and apply it to the *present*, and thus to the *author* of *this* Work."

> "For, contemplate your vocation brothers: that not many philosophers, not many powerful, not many high-born – on the contrary, God has **chosen** the **foolish of the world**, so that He might **shame the philosophic**..."

"Therefore none can boast in the presence of God."

(The Holy Bible in Modern English.
1 Corinthians, 1:26-29 Ferrar Fenton.)

"...how many of you were wise in the ordinary sense of the word, how many were influential people, or came from noble families? No, it was to *shame the wise* that God *chose what is foolish by human reckoning...*"

(The same from The Jerusalem Bible.
All emphases mine.)

Therefore, since I have no academic mandate from a "Theological College" or similar, I will, for the subject matter herein – which greatly derives from The Bible – accept without boast the *greater mandate* from Paul, the appointed Apostle of that time.

This Booklet, substantially derived from **Chapter 5** in the Parent Book: —

BIBLE "MYSTERIES" EXPLAINED:
[Revised Second Edition]
Understanding "Global Societal Collapse" from The "Science" in The Bible;
What Every Scientist, Bible Scholar and Ordinary Man Needs to Know! —

— purposefully offers the revisionist view simply because there are clear and very disturbing discrepancies between the "official theological standpoint" surrounding the life and death of Jesus, and that which The Bible actually states.

Given the fact that the "global Church" comprises so many staunch, unquestioning believers, why should we believe that our analysis of events surrounding the time of Jesus has merit or relevance? After all, literally thousands of books about Jesus, mostly written by very-eminent, intellectual Church scholars and theologians over many hundreds of years, have been produced. How can this little Booklet even dare to stand alongside the heavyweights of the academic/religious world?

Should we view the stated "Church position" as a question of "might being right", and is it therefore also a question of "the greater number must be correct"? Since we unequivocally aver that "The Proof of the Pudding Must *Always* be in the Eating", a key prophetic warning from the Very One Whom the "global Church" rightfully and correctly reveres, offers a very sobering insight into the exact reason for this Booklet, and thus for its challenging stance. From The Book of Matthew, part-verses 21-22:

> "...for there shall then be wide-spread affliction, such as has *not been known* since the *beginning* of the world *until now*, no, nor will *ever* be known again. And if those times were not cut short, ***not a man would be saved.***"

If we state that we accept the words of Jesus and The Bible, should we blithely gloss over His warning as recorded in Matthew, or should we give it serious credence? Most believers will say they accept His words. That being the case, where does that place the two billion Christians currently alive and well on earth? That huge number cannot possibly be the few – the remnant – which is supposed to surmount the time of destruction.

With such a powerful warning, surely a key question arises here. Rational logic should tell us that such a warning would only be given if it could be seen that the greater mass of global humanity ***would fail***. Quite obviously, that number must include very many Christians too. Any view to the contrary would clearly call into question the very mandate of He whom Christians profess to follow and Who clearly possesses the absolute right to so proclaim. How and why, then, would such a terrible failure occur?

Only one answer has credence here! Ultimately it is all about acceptance or non-acceptance of what *actually* is the Truth about everything connected with, and surrounding the Life, Death and *Resurrection* of Jesus. Thus exactly according to **Immutable Divine Law** which inherently *resided* in Him, and which He brought down to sinking humankind.

The warning admonition, **"God is not mocked"**, bluntly means that every nuance of every happening concerned with **His Will** is also not to be mocked. That fact must therefore be unequivocally applied to all events surrounding the life and times of

10

Jesus too. The blind acceptance of teachings that defy rational logic and which therefore transgress what are clearly natural processes – **The Creator in His Divine Perfection being the Absolute of All that is Natural** – means that such beliefs deny the very Perfection inherent in **Him** and **His Will**, of which Jesus was and is Part!

And since Jesus stated that He came "not to overthrow the Law, but to fulfil it", an associated question must logically be: "What Law"; "Whose Law"? It is certainly not human law. It must therefore be **THE LAW** – from out of **THE DIVINE** – purely and logically because that *is* the Origin of Jesus, The Son of God! Precisely because such Perfection of Law cannot possibly be open to human interpretation or opinion, why is it that within the "global Church", diverse and differing opinions and interpretations abound, and all from the same book?

It might be said that we, too, are attempting to do the same, and that this essay is no different, just another interpretation. However, there, in that assumption, the difference ends. For what we are unequivocally postulating is completely at variance with the "cornerstone tenets" of *all* Christian Church communities. Moreover, the explanations herein follow brutally logical paths. Since The Creator's Will and Law cannot possibly be anything *but* logical, only a logical analysis will come closest to divining the true picture, in necessary accordance with The Law!

If we now track back to the warning from Jesus that few will survive the necessary "cleansing process", it again logically follows that *all* incorrect teachings and beliefs surrounding the life and person of Jesus – *irrespective of how or why derived* – must also suffer destruction. For all that is wrong, all that is incorrect, *inherently opposes* the Perfect Will of the Most High, and must therefore be "cast out".

The subject matter and explanations about Jesus in this Booklet, and indeed in the complete Parent Work, therefore unequivocally stands aside and apart from all *religious and academic opinion*.

May the reader find within the clear truth of our assertions!

JESUS! His Birth, Death and Resurrection

> "Do not imagine that I have come to abolish the law and the prophets; *I have not come to abolish but to complete them.*"
>
> (Matthew 5:17, Fenton.)

> "I come to throw *fire* upon the earth; and how I wish *it were already kindled!* ..."

> "Do you imagine that I have come to give peace to the earth? Not at all; *I tell you*, on the contrary, *contention.*"
>
> (Luke 12:49-51, Fenton.
Emphases mine.)

The path humankind should have taken was one that would have ensured a spiritual and harmonious 'paradise on earth'. That path was to have been through the great Truths given to humankind through those men Called for the purpose. Clearly, that did not happen. Even the powerful and sublime intervention of The Son of God Himself still did not induce humankind to genuinely recognise the actual nature of the Perfect Truth He brought. In its place, and founded upon it, we have, instead, just religions – thousands of them. And within all, distortions of that Truth to varying degrees, and all claiming to have the correct interpretation.

Therefore, since we state that we unequivocally accept the Perfection of The Laws of God for all things, by virtue of such a sure conviction within the very broad parameters that Bible *interpretation* currently encompasses [i.e., the broad, easy path]; a critical assessment of two *seemingly* contentious issues in the life of Jesus is imperative.

LAWS: Perfect in their inception, conception and fulfilment. Perfect? Unequivocally yes. And perfect in accordance with the very Laws that Jesus came to fulfil. Any "imperfection" or contention, therefore, will only be "formed" and therefore given life and credence by human opinions and beliefs.

In order to ensure that we do, indeed, possess a clear mandate for what we now state here, let us formulate for ourselves a series of questions to show exactly that. In any case, irrespective of whatever one may choose to believe about the birth, life and death of Jesus, the particular questions posed here must be faced honestly. If not faced thus, then he who still doubts *automatically denies* the inviolable Perfection of The Creator.

1. Question. Can the **"Perfection of God"** be called into question?

   Answer. No!

2. Question. Can a Perfect God produce imperfect Laws?

   Answer. No!

3. Question. If we accept the premise that The Almighty is, and must therefore be, Perfect – by virtue of His Nature – must His Laws of Creation similarly also be Perfect?

   Answer. Yes!

4. Question. If His Laws are Eternal, Inviolable in their Perfection, and therefore Unchangeable, can any event then take place *outside* the parameters of that stated *Inviolable* Perfection?

   Answer. No.

5. Question. Would such an absolute and illogical impossibility reveal believers of any such event to thus be gravely in error?

   Answer. Yes!

6. Question. Would any such beliefs therefore pit themselves *against* the very Laws that The Almighty Himself has ordained for all of Creation?

14

Answer. Yes!

7. Question. If the answers to all our previous questions unequivocally deny **any imperfection** in The Almighty and His Laws, can we still continue to believe that He can change His Perfect Laws at will in order to bring about a particular event?

   Answer. No!

8. Question. If we, nevertheless, still persist in incorrectly believing that He can somehow transgress His Own Perfect Laws to "do as He pleases", would that suggest earthly religious doctrine as being the *fostering agent/s* for such views in order to thereby suit a said dogma?

   Answer. Yes!

9. Question. By virtue of such an inherently flawed concept, can we thus therewith illogically and very incorrectly impute to The Creator – Who must forever innately be **"The Perfect God"** – the *earthly failing* of imperfection?

   Answer. Clearly and unequivocally: – **No!**

Thus, only with such Perfection in The Godhead and The Eternal Laws that have issued from It, could there be a Creation for Jesus to enter in the first place. And, also, by extension within those Creation-parameters, precisely these peculiarly human debates about His so-called 'virgin birth' and, of course, His Crucifixion, Resurrection and Ascension.

By virtue of the only correct answers that could possibly be given to our series of questions, we have gifted ourselves a clear and honest mandate to continue.

0.1 "Virgin" Birth and "Immaculate" Conception

Just as the *physical* death of Jesus at the end of His life marked His exit from earthly life, so did His birth as a baby herald His *physical* arrival onto the earth and into earthly existence. For in accordance with the inviolability of The Divine Laws *He came to fulfil*:

The Son of God could not circumvent The Law that to be born of woman on earth, the seed must first be placed within the womb by a natural procreative event.

Subsequent to impregnation, a lawful gestation period of nine months in that *especial* womb.

Here, however, a singularly contentious question arises with the inescapable truth that in the twin realities of *physical* birth and *physical* death, one must obviously always follow the other. Since the purpose of this essay is to boldly question certain strongly entrenched sacrosanct beliefs in Christian theology, the key one now is the truth or otherwise of the so-called "virgin-birth" of Christ.

Since we cannot deny the fact of Mary's earthly pregnancy or the earthly birth of Jesus as a baby, should we dare to believe that those *earthly* processes might just have been *preceded* by an *earthly* conception too? Or is that going too far? Or is it simply a matter of religious fear masquerading as the "ostensible" guardian of "religious righteousness" standing ready to condemn any attempt to delve logically into what was a completely natural event i.e., Jesus issued, and was delivered, from Mary's womb? Even though a perfectly natural birth, it was, without doubt, one of stupendous import. For it was an incarnation ordained and sanctified by **Divinity Itself.**

Now, because every human spirit incarnating on earth requires a physical vessel in which to dwell and through which to work, Jesus, too, needed a *physical body* to carry out His Work. However, all such bodies must enter the earth plane in baby form from a birth-mother. This is only possible with an earthly conception to begin with.

Does the idea of an earthly conception, then, denigrate the greatness or purity of the person of Jesus or His inherent Divinity? No, of course not. What about the purity of Mary herself, or her exalted Calling? Would we regard her as being somehow soiled or impure if a conception was necessary before Jesus could be born onto the earth? Here, again, of course not.

If we did, it would be very difficult to reconcile the birth of The Son of God from out of a woman of the earth whose necessary purity for that purpose was somehow *compromised* through a *natural* act of copulation **Divinely-sanctified** for **The very One *from* The Divine.**

So, would a possible father for the purposes of a necessary conception debase the body of Mary who would carry to full term the *earthly vessel* that Jesus, *in His Divine reality*, **would inhabit and work through**? For such a high and purely ordained purpose, moreover, might not such a man be similarly **chosen from Above**? And would such a union for that highest possible purpose not therefore constitute an **"immaculate conception"** in the truest sense? If not, why not? If not, would it be because The Bible *appears* to state otherwise?

The birth of Jesus out of Mary must be very correctly regarded as being of the most sublime purity. That correct recognition, however, should not automatically condemn every other mother before or since as being unclean or impure simply because a normal conception was obviously naturally required before a subsequent birth could be realised. If the resultant viewpoint from *some* religious quarters is of that mind-set for all other births, then it is one that is clearly dangerously distorted. For any such misconstrued stance would foolishly denigrate the very ordination of The Almighty in the outworking of His *Perfect Laws* which state that if a man and woman wish to produce offspring in the ordained *natural manner*, they must firstly become **"one"**. Surely no argument there. Even animals have to do that.

In any case, the state of marriage should not necessarily be regarded as the *only* institution under which a child should be conceived. If we fully understand that the inherent key attribute of The Almighty must be Love in its Divine Purity, then the very notion of a *completely pure yet natural process* of conception to birth, as in the case of Jesus, offers the same *potential* for purity for every other human mother too.

A clue to the reason for the wide Christian acceptance of the "virgin birth" as truth may lie in the interpretation by Matthew of the title, the "Holy Spirit". For in 1:20, he reports:

> "...the origin of Jesus the Messiah was thus: Mary, His mother, was promised in marriage to Joseph; but before their union, she was found to have conceived *from* the Holy Spirit. Her husband Joseph, however, was a righteous man; and not wishing to degrade her, felt inclined to divorce her privately. But while reflecting about it, he

saw a messenger from the Lord appear to him during a vision, saying":

"Joseph, son of David, you need not be afraid to accept your wife Mary; for what is conceived in her was **_produced by_** the Holy Spirit:..."

(Emphases mine.)

Because it was so stated by one of the Disciples, it is now forever regarded as sacrosanct in its *apparent* meaning. That is; that the egg – from which the **_physical foetus_** would grow to become the **_physical vessel_**, the **_body_**, **_of Jesus_** inside the womb of Mary – was somehow literally impregnated by "The Holy Spirit" simply to produce **_just the mortal or physical cloak_**.

What needs to be fully understood here once more is that the *mortal cloak* of Jesus **_was not Him_** solely and completely. It was simply **_the body_** that **_housed_** His **_Divine Core_**.[1] We should further understand that the ordained path of *every* physical cloak is to return to the earth out of which it is ultimately constituted. From Ecclesiastes 12:6-7, Fenton. [Italics mine.]

"And man goes to the *earth that he was*, And his Soul will return to the GOD Who gave it!"

It was **_His Divine Core_** – which at the same time **_was He personally_** – which **_returned to become One With the Father_**. The forming of His physical body did **_not_** require the Power of The Holy Spirit to produce it. Physical bodies by the score are produced every day of the week on earth.

However, the *entry* of **Jesus** *down into* the depths of The World of Matter *from out of* the **Highest Heights** of **The Divine Realm**, *to subsequently incarnate* **_into a human foetus on earth_**, clearly **_did_** need **The Holy Spirit** to effect it.

---

[1]Explanations of the processes of Creation that brought forth "both parts to man" i.e., body and spirit, may be read in the Parent Work: **'BIBLE "MYSTERIES" EXPLAINED'**; Chapter 2, **'The Origins of Man: Genesis and Science Agree'**; and a sister Booklet of the same Chapter name. [Available through www.crystalbooks.org]

So one of the keys to a final understanding of this whole question must take into account the true meaning of the Title, **Holy Spirit**, in strict concert with the way that Matthew refers to it for the conception of Jesus. [We will *conclude* this segment with that essential knowledge.]

For the moment, however, two points must be considered if the question of the "virgin-birth" of Jesus is to be finally answered satisfactorily correctly. One is the inviolability and absolute Perfection of The Living Laws of The Almighty, of which we have already made a clear determination. The other is the *true* meaning of the word *conceive*, and of the word, *virgin*.

The Christian Church's imposition of a narrow, intellectual constraint upon the meanings and usage of the words in this particular case fail to understand that:

> *...word meanings relating to activities and ordinations from The Living Light* **must inherently be fundamentally more comprehensive and far-reaching in scope than any earth-orientated faith/belief dogma or doctrine.**

In human thinking the word, conceive, is invariably and immediately associated with pregnancy:

1. 1 a. To become pregnant with. Or:

2. b. To begin or induce the conception of.

However, if we apply other meanings to the word:

3. 2 a. To form in the mind, to become possessed by; Or

4. b. to *formulate*; *devise*: *conceive a plan* – then a far more comprehensive picture is revealed.

(Reader's Digest Great Illustrated Dictionary. Vol. I)

If we now revisit Matthew's narration about this matter, we have the phrase, "***conceived from*** The Holy Spirit"; and a second, "***produced by*** The Holy Spirit". Yes, it could be seen to be "playing with words". But what actually **was** *conceived from* and *produced by* The Holy Spirit here? Other Bibles use slightly different phrasing, but all must *ultimately* mean the same thing, simply because Jesus was born to Mary – under the aegis of the Grace of The Almighty and His Inviolable Laws!

Matthew's narration in The Jerusalem Bible states:

> "...she was found to be with child through the Holy Spirit."

The angel of the Lord then says:

> "...because she has conceived what is in her by the Holy Spirit."

From the King James Bible the same passages respectively read:

> "...she was found with child of the Holy Ghost."

And from the angel:

> "...for that which is conceived in her is of the Holy Ghost."

With such *apparent* clarity, it is eminently clear why so many well-meaning Christians will not even begin to question the so-called "virgin-birth".

Unquestioning loyalty to a high ideal carries a certain measure of greatness. Where it is a matter of The Truth or otherwise of a particular event, "set in motion" by The Living Laws of God, however, then any nominal absolute sureness of the given belief must inherently conform to, and comply with, those very Laws. Any position that does not do so – irrespective of how strong or self-sanctified the belief may be from a human/religious viewpoint – must therefore *set itself against* the **very sanctity** and **Inviolability** of the Perfection of The Laws of God. And therefore against **The Almighty Himself**.

If, however, we accept the idea of a *physical* resurrection and ascension for Jesus, then the current, accepted belief of a *virgin-birth according to Christian theology* **might** make sense. Nonetheless, such an idea would need to somehow accommodate the possibility of a Divine Being from The Realm of The Almighty Himself in some way becoming physical in a kind of **Divine totality** on *earth* through *an actual conception from* that High Source. Using the more logical, more rational meaning of the word, *conceive*, here, inherently encompasses a far greater reality that transcends and transforms narrow earthly parameters.

Thus to *form in the mind*, to *formulate*, to *devise*, to *conceive* – a **plan**, whereby Jesus, The Son of God, would incarnate on earth in a human body. **That** was what was **conceived from**, and **produced by**, The Holy Spirit.

It was an **Immaculate Conception, *conceived* in Plan and Ordination**, and thus ***produced by* The Holy Spirit**!

We should recognise that the term, ***Holy Spirit***, is a ***Divine Title*** relating to a ***specific Being*** of ***Divine Origin***. It is not some kind of amorphous, super-endowed force or power that can perform any act arbitrarily, against the very Laws that are in Him and which He fulfils without flaw or deviation. For that is the meaning of Perfection – without flaw! Therefore, it does not refer to the simple, earthly matter of the impregnation of a human woman, of which there are millions at any given *moment* – but certainly many thousands.

That being the case, it should not be at all difficult to understand that whilst the earthly foetus was formed according to natural processes, ***the entry of The Divine Core of Jesus into that earthly vessel*** was, indeed, carried out **in accordance with The Divine Will through Divine Activity**!

In other words, **The Living, Divine <u>Essence</u> of Jesus, as a <u>Part</u> of God, was brought down to <u>earth</u> from out of the Highest Heights to then <u>enter</u> the <u>vessel</u> prepared for <u>Him</u>** – – the growing ***foetus*** in Mary's womb.
Upon His death, He had then to return to His Origins and become "One with the Father", as He Himself stated. Simple to understand, but truly stupendous as a living happening! And perfectly natural according to The Law He came to fulfil.

In its *earthly* aspect, the historical narrative from the time indicates that in Mary's village, the man with whom she *necessarily* became *'one flesh'* – *precisely to facilitate the 'ordained' pregnancy which would bring forth the **body** for the **Divine Jesus*** – was known to *many*, thus the inclusion of and reference to him in

21

anecdotal records of the period. Indeed, Mary was vilified because of her very brief but *necessary* association with the man *when out of wedlock*, hence Joseph's disquiet. As a devout Jew, Joseph would surely have had no hesitation at all in accepting a woman who was "with child from the Holy Spirit" as his wife. What an incredible honour.

The historical reality, however, simply serves to show the complete naturalness of the whole event in the first place; as it must clearly be if it is to accord with the Perfection of Creation-Law. Thus, the *actual father* was also one *especially chosen*, to thereby *absolutely* ensure an *immaculate* conception for the *pregnancy* which would house **The Divine Core** of **Jesus**.

If we now analyse the meaning of the word, *virgin*, you, the reader, may perhaps *intuitively-recognise* a plain and simple truth in interpretative-logic here too. For even though we believe our previous analyses have offered a clear enough picture of the 'forces' and 'processes' that brought Jesus onto the earth, we should still nevertheless go through this last little exercise in word-meaning.

Thus the accepted meaning in current doctrine regarding Mary, interprets *virginity* and/or the *virgin birth* as stating that **she had not ever had sexual relations with a man.** We must therefore conclude that Mary became pregnant through a method that somehow precluded all the natural processes that The Living Laws of God unequivocally state to be *inviolable*. Such a notion, of course, would have to go against the very Laws that Jesus Himself stated He had come to fulfil.

If we therefore apply broader parameters to the *concept* of virginity in the context of the *complete organic process of childbirth*, then we may begin to discern a far deeper and more natural meaning for the word than is currently applied in the case of Mary. Moreover, if we extend the very essence of the word, *virgin*, and apply it to a *process* that had *not ever come into activity before*, then we can correctly state that *prior to* the particular activity, the key aspects associated with it must have been *virginal*. Within Mary, therefore, the organs of procreation and reproduction were *virginal* for the birth of Christ.

They had not come into activity in this manner prior to that exalted birth.

So a "Virgin Birth" for Jesus <u>was</u> the reality.

22

Thus did Jesus fulfil every last nuance of The Law by which, and for which, He came *down* to the earth!

One final word on this subject: If we are able to grasp the fact that **The Holy Spirit**, both in **Term** and **Title**, is exactly synonymous *with* **The Holy Will**, then we will see that the *true* Title here is **The Will of GOD**.[2] Therefore: The whole process of the entry of **The Son of GOD** onto the earth centres on the nigh incomprehensible nature of **The Love** of **THE ALMIGHTY** Gifting **Jesus** to a *falling* humankind, so that through **Him** we might learn **The Truth** and not fall '*completely*'.

That Divine outworking, however, was *conceived from*, and *produced by*, **The Holy Spirit**. Thus through **He** Who was then, and Who is today, and Who forever will be – **The WILL of GOD:**

IMANUEL!

If the truth of it all was such that God could change His Perfect, Inviolable and thus Unchangeable Laws at will – and therefore somehow permit "imperfection" to arise to suit human religious opinion and interpretation – we should ask ourselves this simple yet brutally-obvious question: "Why did He not place Jesus on earth **as a fully grown man?**"

The need for His babyhood and childhood phase would have been completely obviated. And why could The Almighty not do that? Because the Perfection of His Laws do not, and could not ever, permit such arbitrary happenings. For, in truth, The Laws governing earthly procreation just as naturally also reflect the inviolability of their unchangeable Perfection. This fact offers the absolute premise once again that, even here, *in the conception of the earthly vessel for Jesus*, The Laws *could "not be overthrown"*, as He Himself clearly stated.

An earthly procreation can *only* occur when the natural Laws governing this process are fulfilled, and this was so with Jesus. In

---

[2]The designations, **Holy Spirit** and **Will of God** must be understood as the same **Divine Being**. Full explanations can be read in the Parent Work and in a Sister Booklet titled **The Two Sons Of God**.

the same way that **that** natural act of procreation was spiritually-elevated to especially produce His earthly body, every **normal** sexual act similarly carries the same *potential* for a pure conception too. Unfortunately, however, many conceptions occur as a result of drunkenness, drug use and/or general social debasement, and cannot be considered even remotely pure.

An Especial Note:

If we are *ever* to *truly understand* what this incredibly powerful *sexual-force* is *really for* and how we should *use it correctly*, we need to have *precise knowledge* of the connection, process and outcome. And that is: **'CREATION-LAW' Knowledge!**

For the world reels under the insidious pressure of a multi-billion dollar global industry that promotes sex and more sex in all its forms, both natural and deviant. The drug companies add their billion-dollar earnings contribution as well. What hope for the *average* human to be just *normal*?

The question should thus be asked:

"Why do humans constantly seek greater and greater pleasure in an act that is inherently and naturally extremely pleasurable in the first place?"

Very clearly, global humanity is foolishly-compromised here, for **The Law of Balance** is seriously transgressed; never mind **The Iron Law of Karma** – [**The Law of Reciprocal Action**.][3]

In terms of the 'ennobled-aspect' of sexual intimacy, then: From the Highest **Knowledge-source** ever brought *down* to the earth, we herewith itemise the *primary* considerations. It is *precisely* that **Knowledge-source**, moreover, from which the explanations herein are derived.

1. Just as the needs of the physical body of food, rest, sleep, exercise and bodily elimination in their turn etc., must be satisfied, so should the natural desire for sexual

---

[3]Knowledge of The Spiritual Laws of Creation [**Creation-Law**] is explained in Chapter 3 of the Parent Work; BIBLE "MYSTERIES" EXPLAINED... — and in a stand-alone Booklet.

intimacy. To struggle *against* the *natural* instincts is unhealthy.

2. Fulfilling the natural desire of the body can only *further*, not hinder, the *development* of the *spirit* in the inner [man/woman]; otherwise The Creator would not have placed this desire within us.

3. As with all activities, excesses are harmful. **The Law of Spiritual Balance** must therefore be heeded here too.

4. The *human/material aspect* decrees that the act be undertaken with a fully matured and healthy body; not one *artificially* stimulated or very weakened.

5. The *spiritual aspect*, in necessary concert, decrees thus: That it should only occur; '*...when perfect spiritual harmony has existed between both sexes. And in its consummation, therefore, sometimes strives towards physical union as well*'.

6. So, in clarifying encapsulation: ***'Physical union not only serves to procreate, but from it is furthered the equally valuable and necessary process of an intimate fusion [an inner blending] and a mutual exchange of vibrations, thus producing higher spiritual power.'***

Therein lies the power, purpose, beauty, love and pleasure in the sexual intimacy between man and woman! And therein, also, will be found the great and necessary: **Spiritual Virtue of Trust!**

Notwithstanding the obvious fact that a *natural* level of sensuality will always accompany consensual sex, adhering to the ennobled considerations notated above will *greatly help* any conception to be "immaculate".

In the context of the *reason* for Jesus's birth, however, let us take this argument of the perfection or non-perfection of The Laws to the next obvious step and "allow" God to make us all sinless and perfect, but of course *without* free-will and *personal spiritual responsibility*. There would then have been *no need* for Jesus to come *all the way down* to Earth at all. He would have thus been spared His life of struggle against an intransigent people who, even though awaiting **His** Coming, nevertheless *still murdered Him*.

Thus the words of Jesus in declaring that He had come to "...fulfil the Law", must surely mean exactly that. Without exception, we are all born under The Law, we produce "our works" under The Law, and we die under The Law. Throughout our complete existence, for however long that may be, we receive the "returns of our works", good or bad, under the aegis of The Law.

Let us once more in reinforcement strongly reiterate the fact that since the physical body is *not* the "animating power" of any individual, the "inner animating power" that actually *was* Jesus, was therefore *not that* of His physical body. That was of material substance – 'dust to dust'; thus of the earth. His "inner self" revealed **Itself** *through* the powerful radiations *emanating from* the physical shell He was obliged to take upon entering the material world; in strict accordance with The Eternal Laws He came to fulfil. **The 'Radiating-Power' within Him was of Divine Origin.**

These facts naturally call into question the notion of a *physical* resurrection of Christ. Notwithstanding the many pointers in the previous explanations for the spiritually-perceptive reader to deduce the Truth of what actually occurred here as well, a following section will offer further pointers to a greater clarification of not only the Resurrection, but the Ascension also. [Section 0.3]

0.2   Mission of the "Three Wise Men" [The 3 Kings]

An interesting theme emerges with the whole issue surrounding the birth of Jesus, His subsequent and difficult Mission, and His death as a supposed, necessary, propitiatory sacrifice to cleanse the world and humanity from sin. [That is actually quite a strange and illogical view when looked at brutally-objectively.] Nevertheless, if that *were* the case, what role did the Three Kings or "three wise men" play in the overall picture, in terms of what *they* achieved? More to the point, perhaps, what might have been their *actual* role and mission?

We have their names and, according to recent research, we have a clearer picture of who they were and where they came from

– probably Parthian from the Persian Empire. We also know they travelled for a long time to finally arrive at the birth-place of Jesus. Was this just guesswork? Highly improbable. For how could they know where to go by simply guessing? History informs us that they were wise in the art of astrology – the forerunner of astronomy – and thereby divined the Holy Event. After so much preparation and "guidance" – never mind the long camel/horse journey itself – why, then, just bring expensive gifts to the Child ... and simply ride away?

If, however, we are prepared to consider another and more spiritually-meaningful reason – in terms of so much preparation to locate just one Child, albeit a very special One – then we should reflect on their status to begin with. In the first place they were kings in their own right and so possessed great wealth. Secondly, they were evidently highly regarded as wise men and rulers. And *all three* were carefully and *collectively* guided to find **Him**.

A logical extrapolation of those three points would suggest they were "Called" for that task. History well records the fact that the Mission of Jesus was constantly opposed by the religious authorities of the day who saw in him a danger to *their* authority and who subsequently *succeeded* in their plot to kill Him. That being the case, might it not be possible that the *primary* purpose of those three powerful men was to take Him into their care and protection so that He might carry out His Work relatively unhindered?

Consider how different His mission would have been had the 3 Kings accomplished theirs'. In the first place, it would not have been so tragically cut short. Under their protection His sublime Commission would have unfolded to its utmost point, which was *not* death by crucifixion. Given that the Three Kings recognised Him as The One sent from Above, we would further expect that royal scribes would probably have been appointed to record His every Word; all His Teachings. How different the "Christian world", particularly, would be today. However, because the three monarchs failed to recognise their *true Calling* and task, what we subsequently have as a result of that unfortunate error is a more fractured, divided and divisive "Christian religion" than perhaps would otherwise have been the case had Jesus received that protection.

It may not ultimately have prevented a violent death at some point in His life, but a strong blanket of royal protection from the "Three Kings" *might* have induced certain religious authorities to tread more carefully with regard to His Person. At the very least we might have had historical access to a far longer Ministry by Him with perhaps His Teachings eventually recorded by Him personally. Of course, in terms of what actually occurred, it is all supposition. Interestingly, many who are religiously-inclined subscribe to a rather strange view which states that *if* a particular thing takes place, it does so because it *must automatically be* **The Will of God**. That particular notion completely fails to understand that human beings have *free will* in **all** matters. Therefore, the path of a prophet, or even of a Son of God, can either be helped or hindered by those who might cross that path – including and especially The Three Kings.

By not placing Jesus under their care and protection – even though clearly guided to find and acknowledge him as the Awaited One – they nonetheless ultimately hindered His Mission. Not purposely or from dark intent, but rather *through not fully recognising their primary purpose.* The fact that Herod – fearing the prophecy about the "King" who would be born in his time and ordering the slaying of all male children up to the age of two years – surely reveals that the true purpose of the "Three Kings" in their ordained journey **was** to find and *protect* the Child.

The warning from the Messenger of God to Mary and Joseph to flee from Herods wrath to Egypt surely reinforces the fact of our statement. A human failing of severe proportions necessitated direct and rapid intervention from The Light to ensure that The Son of God's Mission would not be cut short by a vengeful despot, with obviously severe ramifications for future humanity. Had Herod succeeded in killing Him as a baby, the world today would be completely bereft of the essential knowledge He gave to the world. Even though his Teachings have suffered terrible distortions; they have, for the most part, *still* shown the way forward for many. Without them, an ongoing, more or less permanent, "Dark Age" would probably have been the resultant horror.

The Three King's, ***through their great error***, unfortunately bequeathed to future Christians and the world, ongoing contention about the Life and Mission of Jesus. And thus even the very issues we address in *this* Booklet. The *apparent* final resting place of those three men – or at least their skulls [revered and crowned in gold and precious stones] – is the Cathedral of Cologne. According to the 'Christian historical record', that Cathedral was especially constructed to house those very relics.

0.3   Resurrection and Ascension

The Resurrection and Ascension of Jesus must surely rank as one of the most religiously contentious issues ever. Science, by virtue of its empiricist base, would quite rightly reject notions of the *physical resurrection* of a dead body. Science would probably also reject the idea of *ascension*, physical or otherwise. In bygone days, any opposition to the once all-powerful church position that Jesus was resurrected physically, would certainly have bought an immediate death sentence and execution. Yet the very Scripture we use as the introduction to this particular Essay clearly states that precise rules hold unequivocal sway for all, including The Son of God Himself Whose words we accept they are.

Physical resurrection and ascension! What should reason and objective logic tell us about it?

For we are surely enjoined by The Living Law Itself to employ what all humans are gifted with, the attribute to think and weigh with intelligence, logic and reason. If forcibly locked into either an earthly empirical or a fundamentalist or religious framework, the issue under discussion here might appear to be satisfactorily validated for some, or perhaps even for many.

In the final analysis, however, an event such as a *physical* resurrection and ascension, which radically departs from "natural" processes, cannot be held up as being logical in any way whatsoever. Correct clarification, therefore, must inherently rely on the truth and outworking of the very Laws that Jesus Himself stated could not be overthrown. And which He, according to the lawful parameters thus contained within them, also had to submit to at **His** death.[4]

Because our mandate derives from the Perfection of The Spiritual Laws, we can also now seriously question and challenge the second crucial part of this particular belief: i.e., the strong, entrenched notion within probably most Christian communities that a *physical* resurrection and ascension can *somehow* be valid. To this end a key question needs to be asked with regard to the "resurrection" of Jesus: Can a man, any man, in a flesh and blood

---

[4]The full explanation of the *processes* surrounding *earthly death* may be read in the Parent Work.

physical body, weighing somewhere around 70 to 80 kilograms, per-haps – and very surely pronounced dead – realistically rise from that dead state to then live some kind of **physical** reality, eter-nally?

Whilst we certainly accept that Jesus was able to call the dead to life, it was done so under the strictest aegis of The Living Law, of Which He Himself Was and Is a Living Part.

If we therefore employ the knowledge of Spiritual Law to apply the processes of death to the fate of Jesus, we are left with His irrefutable statement – that we must often reiterate – that He had *not* come "to overthrow the Law, but to fulfil it". Not just to fulfil it to a somehow convenient earthly-belief level, but to fulfil it *completely*.

> That being the case He, also, was *absolutely sub-ject* to the *natural* and therefore *lawful processes* of the *normal exit* of His personal, **Divine**, *inner animating core* from the mortal, *physical*, body He was obliged to take upon **being born of a woman of earth.**

So if we now track to the end of Jesus's life, the extremely tenuous rationale offered to ostensibly support a "physical resur-rection" has always been that He *had* to have risen in a physical body – **simply because His own was not in the tomb in which He was placed.**

In its supposed "reasoning" such a one-dimensional view is akin to **medieval superstition.** Quite clearly, Jesus *had no choice but to vacate* His broken, bleeding and dying body on that "cross of death" when His time of exit thereupon arrived. Jesus died a *physical* death, as *all* who are *born* onto the *earth* must.

The Perfection of The Laws of God[5] simply do not allow for

---

[5]The explanations on the inviolability and Perfection of **"The Laws of Creation'** in the **Parent Work** about the 'calling of the dead to life" by Jesus offer a fuller, clearer understanding of the issue under discussion here. The Booklet: **"Whither Cometh Humankind" The Origins of Man** *Genesis and Science Agree"*; similarly offers explanations for understanding the stand-point upon which we base the *what* and *why* of our assertions, and thus the *portent* of this particular segment.

anything other than complete naturalness in all things. **His** Perfect Laws thus represent the *ultimate* level of pure naturalness. Therefore, whereas the inner core of human beings is that of spirit, corresponding to the point or Realm of our origin, the inner core of Power *that actually was Jesus* was, and is, **Divine** – precisely corresponding to His Origins from out of The Godhead.

We know that after His death Jesus was taken down from the Cross and buried in a tomb owned by Joseph of Arimathea. What do we read post-Crucifixion, however? That even those closest to Him *did not recognise Him when He appeared before them*. Mary *did not recognise Him to begin with*. Mary Magdalene, too, *did not recognise Him immediately*. Even two of His Disciples on their way to Emmaus *did not recognise Him for hours* even though *He walked and spoke with them*. How could it be possible that after a short interval of *just days*, those closest to Him *did not recognise Him immediately*? What does this clearly infer?

> It unequivocally infers that had He been in His ***physical*** body, ***recognition would have been immediate.*** Therefore, and in concert with the lawful outworking of the earthly death process, it is obvious that it must have been ***another and different body they saw***.

The theological idea that it was His "transmuted physical body" they saw is not correct, for The Laws of Creation do not permit the "transmutation" of a physical body for anyone; not even in a "one-off" situation for The Son of God. That is The Law! The exit of the "inner being" – the actual "life-force" that is the ***real*** person – from the "physical-body part" means that ***that*** material part is then irrevocably subject to the normal and natural disintegrating process which every physical form must subsequently undergo.[6]

---

[6]The "substitution-premise" that some writers and theologians hold dear, seemingly answers the question of: "Which body was it?" For them, the answer to most of the issues surrounding the Crucifixion and Resurrection seem only to make sense if there was a *substitute* for Jesus on the Cross. Some researchers point to Simon of Cyrenaica as that substitute. Jesus was even supposed to have watched His own "death-walk" hidden from sight. Or that He survived the actual Crucifixion, then later on left the Holy Land

The Laws of Creation decree that a less dense envelope or body is able to penetrate denser objects. The sudden appearance of Jesus inside locked rooms in which the Disciples regularly gathered thus testifies to the fact that He could *not* have been in a *physical body*. It is not lawfully possible to "rarefy" a physical body. Physical bodies cannot penetrate material doors or walls. Not His physical body, therefore, but one that we all possess too.

A non-physical **Ethereal body** of the **consistency** of *that Realm* **through which we journeyed** to incarnate on earth. And, unless through our own *aspiritual* deeds we remain *trapped* in "the world", the *same* Realm through which we *all* must journey again – *'if we wish to return home'*. It is a body, moreover, **that can exist on the earth** – hence the millions of earth-bound souls.[7]

This "other-body" thus answers the question of *how* Thomas could *feel* the wounds of Jesus. It is simply a matter of **the same kind of body within Thomas** i.e., of the **same consistency**, bearing witness to the world of this lawful event. Thomas was *invited* to "touch" and "feel" surely because he was "Thomas the doubter".[8] That being the case, an obvious question begs an answer here.

What really *did* happen to the physical body of Jesus?

We know that guards were posted outside the tomb to prevent the theft of it. Therefore, the story goes, it could not possibly have been stolen, for thieves would have been seen. So the only possibility left is that **we all meekly submit to the belief that Jesus did rise from the dead in His physical body.** And that apparently seems to satisfy the majority of Christians in their various Churches.

Of course, the other logical possibility must not ever be entertained **lest the whole, carefully nurtured, structure totters**

---

with His "wife" to live elsewhere on the planet; France or Britain.

[7]These are the departed who are ignorant of the path they should take and who therefore, of course, are *not* meant to be earth-bound.

[8]Interestingly, Thomas's fulfilment of his amazing mission to India after that must surely be seen to be one of *transformed conviction* from a previously doubting nature.

and comes crashing down. For the reality is that soldiers on sentry duty *do fall asleep,* or they can be bribed to turn a blind eye. Or perhaps the sentries, in strict concert with The Law under The Will of The Almighty, were rendered unconscious for a time, to thereby graciously permit a few especially chosen ones to quietly remove the body so that it might be placed where it would *never ever fall into unbelieving hands.*

Thankfully a small but steadily growing body of religious scholars now subscribe to this "probability", and that His Resurrection and Ascension was thus a "spiritual" event, not a physical one. Deriving their ideas from historical narrative and ancient texts quite recently discovered but ignored by mainstream Christian Churches, this newly-emerging and *correct view* is exactly that which we state in the previous paragraph – that Jesus was moved from His temporary burial chamber and placed in a secret, permanent vault.[9]

For if that particular scenario is regarded as impossible, as blasphemy or heresy even, then we have a *major and insurmountable problem* with the fact that Jesus had to subsequently *return* to The Father. To thus levitate and ascend in that same supposedly *physical body* to a *Realm* that is obviously *non-physical.* And, moreover, to a level far beyond the incomprehensible reaches of the farthest universes even. Such an idea simply beggars description, for it is implausible in the extreme. In fact:

"It is patently impossible!"

As He stated to his Disciples, He would one day leave the earth and become, again, **One with The Father.** In the light of His sure statement, the question that must be put to the whole issue of 'The Ascension' is:

---

[9]The *ostensible* discovery of the ossuary of Jesus in a tomb which also *ostensibly* housed the ossuaries of most of his immediate family members has brought forth the notion that His bones were later recovered from the second chamber to be placed in the "family tomb" as per Jewish tradition. Israeli archeological authorities, very tightly controlling this "discovery", have not allowed any public examination of the bones. For if they *really were* actually those of Jesus, *then precise and particular aspects about certain of His bones would rock Christianity to the core.* [That particular and crucial knowledge *about* the body of Jesus is *revealed* further on in this Booklet.]

"What is the natural reality of God?"

Human beings, of course, cannot *ever* answer that particular question. We cannot possibly know in any kind of "experiential-way" anything *above* our particular origins. By asking that question, however, *we are not seeking an actual answer to it.* We are simply, yet graphically, illustrating the fact that a huge and fundamental problem exists with any belief that Jesus ascended to become One with The Father *in His physical body.*

Do we therefore also believe that The Almighty sits down to a meal? Or that He must subsequently use a toilet, as we must in the physical world? Of course not. It is an utterly ludicrous thought, and one certainly leading towards the blasphemous.

> *However, that kind of physical reality must be accepted as inescapable for anyone who persists in the patently absurd notion that Jesus ascended in His <u>physical</u> body.*

He said often enough:

> "My Kingdom is *not* of this world." "I come into the world and I leave the world."

What is so difficult to understand here? His Kingdom was not of the physical world that we presently occupy. It was of a non-material reality – above the heavens even!
If such a simple reality cannot then be grasped, and one still persists in the belief of a physical-body ascent, then the next question is:

> "At what point or level in the ascent did the necessary transition from a *physical* form to a *non-physical* one take place, **in order for The Son of God to become <u>One</u> with God The Father?**" And: "How much food did Jesus take for the return journey?"

Staunch Christians may regard such questions as a mockery or a defilement of an ostensibly sacred or holy belief. If so, then it is clearly a closed-spirit viewpoint. For the questions posed are extremely valid and must be honestly answered if any actively promoted, conceptual belief of a *physical-body* resurrection *and* ascension is to hold any credibility whatsoever. For one *must* follow the other in terms of any credible physical-mode answer.

This particular distortion may possibly derive, wholly or in part, from an incorrect interpretation about the fate of the dead at the end-time. This belief *ostensibly* states, that then:

"All the dead shall be awakened."

This sentence as it stands conjures up horror-filled images of all the dead emerging from their graves and somehow being fleshed out to physical specifications conforming to their original bodily appearance. And presumably to the same level of knowledge and belief they possessed when they died. How they could ever possibly understand the why of the very different world they will supposedly enter after emerging from their earthly graves, no one seems to have answered. And how can they?

For what about Christians who have been cremated, and whose ashes – at the deceased's wish – have been scattered in more than one location, or even at sea? Fish food. Surely problematic is the question of the hundreds of thousands of believers – including Church martyrs – burnt to ash by marauding armies over centuries. Problematic, also; the very many *true believers* burnt at the stake by the twisted "Dark Ages religious madness" of the very Church that should have protected them. Ash given to the earth becomes just dirt. That reality is **The Law — CREATION-LAW!**
No chance of reassembly there.

The whole idea in its continued belief to the present is nothing more than just latter-day religious madness stemming from Christian fundamentalism's fear and ignorance. Fear of *their interpretation* of **'Judgement-Day'**, and ignorance of the *true* meaning of the particular Scripture of the so-believed 'awakening dead'. In this case, therefore, what has been so terribly distorted over centuries by such wrong thinking is **not** the meaning of the prophecy in the first place.

It is not even the correct wording.

It is not that *"all **the** dead"* shall be awakened but that:

"All <u>that is dead</u> shall be awakened!"

A huge and fundamental difference emerges with the removal of just one word and the inclusion of two others. Those two simple words are crucially-decisive; for the **now correct** Scripture immediately conjures up a more **accurate** picture. **All that is spiritually dead shall be <u>forced</u> to awaken.** This does not at all refer to, or mean, those who have long since died, it means literally **everything** that has not adjusted itself to the correctness of **CREATION-LAW**. Everything that has not voluntarily adjusted itself to **The Law** will thus be *forcibly awakened* to thereby reveal its true nature.

Social structures, concepts, attitudes, religions, families, Nations etc., will be affected according to the level of compliance or non-compliance of The Law previously undertaken prior to this crucial point. At this present time we can observe this "awakening and revelatory process" in such diverse activities as are practised within the corporate world and in Churches and religions. By extension, the previously hidden activities of leaders and senior persons within them will also be subject to this severe and relentless spiritual sifting process.

Nothing will escape this now quite necessary and long-ordained spiritual cleansing. Not one thing, organisation or activity is, or will be, exempt. The perceptive reader should now readily understand the great gulf between a belief that *incorrectly says* "all **the** dead", and one that *correctly states*:
"All **that is** dead"!

Since we have presented a logical explanation of events pertaining to the birth and death of Jesus, it is interesting to note the many attempts to deny His Divinity; that He was just an ordinary man. Should we once more tiresomely reiterate the absolute fact that all born onto the earth must use the form ordained for that purpose, the physical form of either man or woman? There, we have! That is the sole purpose the body serves. It is simply the vessel, the cloak, the overcoat that the life-force in each and every one of us needs as an habitation for *physical life – down here*.

So simple a concept, and so perfect. Yet it provides such fertile ground for scenarios that are so ridiculously impossible that one wonders how the authors could have possibly thought them up. The truly amazing thing about "other-body" realities is that the time eventually arrives for each one of us to be forcibly thrust into exactly that separating-out process we call earthly death. So was it for Jesus too.

Then, *yes then*; through the experience dawns the realisation for most that they had wasted their lives on things that really did not matter, but would now cause them major problems in their non-earthly body. In any case, the academic world's seeming pre-occupation with Jesus and his earthly physicality *completely misses the point* of the whole quite stupendous event – His entry onto the earth as a very necessary act of "Truth-bringing".

"Heed <u>The Word</u>, not the Bringer", should be the primary consideration. In the very first instance it is ***what*** He brought, His Teaching, The Truth inherent in His Divine Core, which should always have been *the first* and *principal thing* to be understood. It was precisely His Word, and not Him *personally* as a "man among men", that was, and is, ***decisive for all on earth***.

What we have today, however, is a virtual cult based on the "personality of Jesus". Evangelical Christians promote the rather strange idea of the necessity for a "personal relationship" with a Power that human beings could not even approach. After His earthly death He warned Mary Magdalene not to touch Him. Having exited His physical body the Power that was always inherent in Him from birth ***was no longer constrained by the heavier physical body***. His Power therefore radiated much more strongly from Him. Even as a "man among men", the Power was still sufficient to effect healing from solely the radiations emanating from just His physical "covering".

Unfortunately for the Christian Church mainly, but for all of humanity ultimately, the true meaning and purpose of His coming from the Highest point in the ***non-material***, Eternal part of Creation all the way down to the lowest point of the ***non-eternal***, material earth has not ever been understood correctly. And to teach that a ***physical body*** can somehow rise to the ***Highest part of the non-material, Eternal Divine Realm*** is surely the ultimate blasphemy.

<u>Blasphemy</u>: it is the word that Christians are often wont to use against those whom they believe denigrate their ostensibly sacrosanct interpretations of Bible Scripture.

I am sure we all accept that The Laws of God are sacrosanct. We would probably further accept that their outworking must be so too. Therefore, in concert with Jesus' serious admonition that He had come to "fulfil The Law" – the reciprocal outworking of which

37

is clearly explained in the Parent Work – what fate must await the Christian Church and its followers for continuing to promote a belief that is not only completely *illogical*, but absolutely *wrong?* The Law *will bring without fail* the commensurate reciprocal consequences to all who would dare to denigrate the **Perfection of The Law!**

So here, in concert with that Perfect Law, we, *now*, both ask and answer the key question:

"What really did happen to the body of Jesus?"

Well, should humankind ever be *permitted to find* the **actual location** of His earthly cloak, the many who have written about Jesus and The Holy Grail and have propounded final resting places in locations as diverse as India, Pakistan and even the South of France – and certainly all Christians who believe He ascended to His **non-material** *Eternal Home* in some kind of transfigured *earthly body* – will then know that they were **all very, very wrong!** The approaching and inevitable appearance in the sky of the **Sign** of The Son of Man will produce the same recognition; and very much more besides.

So, what, exactly, will be revealed to the world should humankind ever be *permitted* the discovery of the exalted earthly body of Jesus, and how will we know that it truly is He? What we herewith present in this Booklet, and of course in the Parent Work, are the keys that will provide the clearest revelation that, *prior* to any such discovery, it will be *"proof positive"* that *it is* the *earthly cloak* of Jesus.

For notwithstanding the *ostensible* archeological "discoveries" of the ossuaries of Jesus and His extended family, any sure conclusion that it might be Him must take into account *certain absolute facts about particular bones of any skeleton stated to be His*.

Therefore, in revelatory clarification: The body that served The Son Of God rests in a sealed cavern under Jerusalem. At the entrance to the cave three crosses are engraved over the right hand arch. The body inside will show evidence of crucifixion, *but the bones in the legs* are

38

not broken. In the row of upper teeth in the skull, *an eye-tooth is missing.* And on the gravestone which covers His body is engraved a specific sign or mark: – **His Sign!**

The missing eye-tooth is obviously singularly significant. But why would we emphasise the fact that the legs on this especial body are not broken? Aside from just the historic aspect of crucifixion as a common method of punishment in Roman life and culture, the reason for such an emphasis relates to the crucial recognition that all of humankind will one day ultimately be forced to make about the true nature, the life, and singular 'Crucifixion of Jesus': – **The Son of God!**

The particular agony associated with crucifixion centres around the fact that being suspended from nailed palms or wrists means; that to prevent compression of the lungs and subsequent asphyxiation, the naturally-sagging body must be held erect. However, as one can readily note when gymnasts perform the "crucifix position" on "the Rings", only the strongest and fittest men in very good health and in their prime can hold such a position for any length of time.

Therefore, the very position of the arms affixed in that "crucifix position" in an *actual crucifixion* means that it is virtually impossible for crucified and probably tortured men to do so. What they could and did use, however, is the leverage point that the *nailed feet* offer. It is the only means whereby the crucified one can relieve the crushing effect of a sagging body – in effect, to push up, to stand, on that driven-through spike.

The burial Laws at the time required that bodies of Jews crucified on the Sabbath be taken down and buried before sunset, so the breaking of the legs ensured a quicker end on that **"Cross of Torture"**.

The Book of John, Chapter 19, Verses 31-37, provides a clear account of that part of the process. (Emphases mine.)

"The Judeans, therefore, since it was preparation-day – for that day was the Great Day of the Week of Rest – so that the bodies might not remain on the cross on the Sabbath, requested Pilate that they might be removed after their legs were broken. The soldiers, therefore, came and broke the legs of the first, as well as of the other one crucified with him; but when they came to Jesus, and seeing that He was already dead, *they did not break His legs.* One of the soldiers, however, with a spear pierced His side; when blood and water issued from it.

"And the eye-witness gives this evidence, and his evidence is truthful; and he himself knows that he speaks true, so that you may believe. For these events happened, in order that the Scripture might be verified: A BONE OF HIM SHALL NOT BE BROKEN."[10]

In that last capitalised sentence (Fenton Bible) lies the key to any so-called "discovery" of the body of Jesus, for it *must show* signs of crucifixion. At the very least, therefore, there will be damaged foot bones from the driven spikes – *but the legs will not be broken.* [So far, the Israeli Archaeological Authority has not agreed to any close examination of the bones in question and, indeed, is unlikely to do so.]

0.4   Jewish Condemnation of The Son Of God

Now: What of that group of human beings who first hailed Him with 'Hosannas', as The Messiah ? And then later shouted: "Crucify him!" They, the Jewish people, called to receive The Son of God in their midst. Where do they *fit* within the outworking of Spiritual Law which ordains that all transgressions against The Divine Will must be expiated to their final point of resolution? The

---

[10]Fenton obviously understood the great importance of the last sentence in John's Scripture for it is Capitalised. [That is not the case with some Bibles.]

historical record clearly shows that the Jewish authorities continually sought the death of Jesus, to the degree of fabricating lies about Him. The legal term today is "entrapment".

The failure of the Three Kings to recognise that their mission was to protect Him set in motion the train of events that would finally bring about His murder. As previously noted, Herod ascertained from the Magi the exact time the star made its appearance and instructed them to learn all they could about the child and report back to him. However, having been instructed by a dream not to return to Herod, they returned to their own lands by another road. Furious at being tricked and fearing the prophecy that a King had been born there, Herod ordered the killing of all newborn male children at the time of Jesus' birth up to the age of two years.

Upon the instructions of a "messenger of the Lord", Joseph and Mary immediately journeyed to Egypt to escape the reach of Herod. Upon Herod's death years later, Joseph was then directed "...to go into the land of Israel." Unfortunately, surely due to his long absence in Egypt, the powerful events of the exalted night of the Divine birth in Bethlehem slipped from Joseph. Along with Joseph and Mary, all who experienced those events then were meant to have borne *stronger witness to it for the world* during their lives. As previously explained, the Three Kings, *called* to be the primary witnesses for all time, **would have changed the course of history then and forever had they fulfilled their primary task of protecting the child.**

The non-recognition of Jesus as the prophesied Messiah by the Jews – *who waited for Him then and are still waiting for a Messiah today* – hinged on the fact that the prophecy about Him correctly named Bethlehem as the town in which the Messiah was to be born. However, Jesus became known as "the Nazarene", for that is where Joseph lived – in Nazareth. Could the Jewish people state such an error to be a simple and legitimate mistake, and therefore not expect any repercussions from the whole, terrible series of events at some future time? Ordinarily, that might possibly possess some saving grace – it was just a mistake.

The Book of John, however, in recording the arrest of Jesus, reveals what was surely the murderous attitude of many within the Sanhedrin toward "the troublemaker".

"The troops, then, headed by their colonel, and the Judean officers, arrested Jesus, and having bound Him, they conducted Him in the first instance to Annas; because he was the father-in-law of Caiaphas, who was high priest for that one year. Now it was Caiaphas who advised the Judeans that *"It is profitable for one man to die on behalf of the people."*

(John 18:13-14 Fenton.
Emphasis mine.)

In this case, therefore, the stakes are crucially higher. What might be now dismissed as a "simple mistake" was, in truth, a hypocritical calculation to get rid of Jesus. That action resulted *in the torture and murder of an innocent man* in the first instance. That in itself is wrong. Secondly and crucially, that particular *murder* was against The One Who, gifted in Love and Grace from The Creator, *came to help humankind out of the mess it had mired itself in.* But Who then, however, was *rejected* by the very people who were called from the time of Moses to prepare for His Coming. Is that not incredibly arrogant and foolish?

If there was, or is yet still to be, severe reciprocity from that repulsive act of blind hatred against The Light Itself, what form might it take? *Or might it just perhaps have already occurred?* We should note here the discourse of Pilate to the baying crowd, and their replies to him. From Matthew 27: 22-25 in Fenton's Bible. [Emphasis mine.]

"What then," asked Pilate, "shall I do with Jesus, Whom they call the Messiah?" "Let Him be crucified!" was their unanimous reply.

"Why?" he asked; "what crime has He committed?" In reply, they yelled out more savagely than before, "Let Him be crucified!"

Pilate ...took water and washed his hands in the presence of the mob, saying, "See, I am innocent of the blood of this just Man; look to it yourselves!"

Then in reply to him, the whole mass shouted out, **"Let His blood be upon us <u>and upon our children!"</u>**

And so Pilate handed Jesus over to be crucified.

In that last terrible and hate-filled imprecation, the inviolable outworking of the very **Commandments** given to that race by their great Patriarch, **Moses the Law-Giver**, began their silent and long-reaching work. The Jewish race: Called to lead the way for humankind with the greater knowledge of **Creation-Law** brought to them by The Son Of God Himself. Through the elucidation of them by Jesus *in their very midst* and thus under His initial guidance, they could have succeeded. Burdened with religious ritual that held them fast to the 'letter' of Jewish law, they failed in their task, for they did not want it.

Because of *that* murder, the ancient prophecy that foresaw the death of Jesus was fulfilled. Not, however, because it was the Will of God that it be fulfilled, but because it could be prophetically seen that *the Jewish people would go against the very laws and prophecies they were meant to obey.*

Thus that failure was prophesied long before Jesus came onto the earth!

So, what can we deduce from the events of 2,000 years ago for those who shouted:

"Crucify Him!"

The Book of Luke records the Admonition of Jesus to "The Daughters of Jerusalem" as he was led to Golgotha.

And a large crowd of the people followed Him, including women, who were beating their breasts, and lamenting Him. Jesus, However, turning towards them, said, "Daughters of Jerusalem, weep not for me; but weep for yourselves and for your children. For now the days are coming, during which they shall say, 'Happy are the barren, happy the childless, and happy those who have

43

never nursed.'[11] Then they will begin to SAY TO
THE MOUNTAINS, 'FALL UPON US'; AND
TO THE HILLS, 'BURY US'; because if they do
this with the green tree, what must happen to
the rotten one?"

(Luke 23: 26-31, Fenton.)

The *'immutable'*, thus *'absolute'*, **Laws of Creation** offer clear
explanations of *all* The Laws and their outworking. They provide
the keys for greater understanding of reciprocity for the murder of
Jesus which we examine at this point in our story.[12]

Bible prophecy and Scripture thus speak of the fact that "...gen-
erations shall not pass until *all* has been fulfilled". We further
know that our works or deeds *must* follow us *after* earthly death.
– *"Their works shall follow them."* – And, under the aegis
of the great **Law of Reciprocal Action** [*what we sow we reap*]
and **The Law of Rebirth**, many centuries may pass before *exactly* the right time and circumstances converge for expiation of
the long-committed deed. Therefore, the notion that "crimes of
enormity" committed against certain races throughout history are
always committed against *innocent* people does not at all corre-
spond with the perfect and inviolable outworking of **The Laws of
Creation**.

---

[11]His warning to the women who lamented Him at that specific
time has been interpreted by some Bible "scholars" as a warning
about the impending wholesale slaughter of Jerusalem's inhabitants under the Roman Commander, Titus. However, what we
should read here is *a larger warning* from The Son of God that
The Law of Reciprocal Action would reach down through the centuries *to all the women and mothers of the world who reject
The Living Word*; The Law that we must all, in the final and
absolute analysis, embrace in gratitude and therefore live by. For
we can clearly see, if we wish to, the ramifications of His severe
warning to women at the end-time. "Woe to the woman who is
with child and who give suck [at the breast...]" A full explanation
may be read in the Parent Work (See end of Booklet) Chapter
3: **The Spiritual Laws** *The Necessary Knowledge* sub-heading;
"Why there is so much Violence and Evil on Earth", .

[12]The key Law here is **The Law of Reciprocal Action** – the
outworking of which is explained in the Parent Work in Chapter 3.

The concept or claim of innocence for dark deeds committed can be used for at least two reasons:

1. Ignorance and/or disbelief of any inviolable and thus constraining Laws to begin with.

2. The recognition that inviolable Laws may or do exist, that the consequences of dark actions are inevitable, but that any potential for a "possible guilt aspect" may hold at bay, even subconsciously, acknowledgement and thus *acceptance* of the long-committed deed.

The obvious ramifications that such *inviolable* Laws presuppose for the individual or group in the necessary expiation of particularly heinous deeds, such as the murder of One from out of The Godhead, means that The Law will, without fail, one day "visit the appropriate reaping" on such a group.

"Ignorance is bliss!" But is it really? In terms of expiating past transgressions, ignorance of The Laws of Creation does not stop their sure outworking. Ignorance or disbelief, therefore, **cannot stay** the reciprocal return. The same applies to the second point. Knowledge of, but refusal to accept, the lawful reciprocity of dark deeds may add **more suffering** to the **inevitable reaping** for the **deed perpetrated** than otherwise might have been the case. The darker and more savage the act, the **stronger** will be the "lawful return". In the case of serious transgressions by **whole peoples**, it naturally follows that the group as a whole *may*, at a future time, **"yet reap together"**.

However, due to the lawful outworking of The Laws of "Rebirth...", "Attraction..." and "Reciprocal Action...", it does not necessarily follow that the group present at a particular event in history that must require expiation – such as the murder of Jesus – will all incarnate together at a given future point for that expiation to occur. *Yet they may.* In any case, unless the individuals present at the event who *did* contribute in even the *smallest* way to the deed **had not come to recognition of their part in it since that time**, then the long reach of the Justice of The Law would require them to be back on the earth around the time it was ordained that **all karmaic cycles must close.**

However, in the case of the murder of Jesus, it is not only those who shouted: "Crucify Him", who will 'reap the appropriate return', but all human beings who have rejected Him and The Living Truth He brought to humankind. With those directly and indirectly involved in the actual, incomprehensible event – those who took part in his murder and those who were willing servants of the plotters and planners – all would need to be on earth when **The Son of Man** proclaimed His presence. And therewith to recognise Him through the **All-Truth** He would bring which would clarify *The Truth* surrounding *the life* and *true Mission* of Jesus, **The Son of God**. Recognition of that crucial Truth by the perpetrators and supporters could *thereby* bring expiation for them.[13]

Since all karmaic cycles have been closing rapidly for some time now but more exponentially in the present – hence the "increasing reaping" everywhere on earth today – we should yet note how history records countless events where various races perpetrated horrific acts against others. In those kinds of unfortunate episodes in human history, we may thereby better understand the inviolable aspects of The Law.

World War II saw perhaps the greatest ever concentration of dark deeds perpetrated against many races in many different parts of the globe. The world also witnessed the curious phenomenon of mass non-responsibility from the citizens of the main perpetrating groups. They gave as their excuse or reason; they were just "following orders", or had no choice – particularly where they were led by a megalomanic/charismatic leader. In any Nation or race, however, the inviolable outworking of The Law does not absolve any person – who simply "follows a leader into mad savagery" – of personal responsibility.

The "one-life-only" school of thought, which does not take into account the lawful outworking of precise and inviolable Laws, will naturally describe those on the receiving end of "crimes of enormity" as *innocent victims*. The reality is, however, that what has taken place under the aegis of **The Laws of 'Rebirth', 'Attraction...'** and **'Reciprocal Action'** is simple *reciprocity*; – "What we sow, that shall we reap" in the first instance. So races and peoples who continually lament that they are the 'victims' need to recognise, understand and accept that **The Law** does not deliver injustice. That is impossible. At this rapidly-closing time of

---

[13]The Christian reader, particularly, should very seriously strive to spiritually absorb the contents of Chapter 12, **"The Two Sons of God"**, of the Parent Work:. **In truth, however, the crucial knowledge about "The Two Sons of God" is for every human being on earth and in the beyond. In short, for all!**

humankind's odyssey, people and races receive or *"reap"*, simply because **they once "sowed the seed"**.

The horrific experience of the Jewish people at the hands of the Nazi Regime during the Holocaust brought forth strong statements from some survivors about whether or not there could be a God. Anecdotal evidence from 'camp-survivors', particularly from Auschwitz immediate post-liberation, noted liberated Jews proclaiming: "There is no God." Some survivors interviewed in recent times still held to that belief.

On the surface, such a view may be perfectly understandable given the years of traumatic suffering some survivors underwent at that particular "death-camp". However, if analysed logically, such comments are really silly in the extreme for they seek to **blame God** for **all** human misfortune. Moreover, the same comments ultimately incorporate, and thus focus on, a too-strong emotive/cultural overtone centred on a people with a strong religious history of being regarded – in their own eyes – as "chosen by God".

So in terms of that nonetheless horrific episode in Jewish history, do we seriously believe that it was The Creator Who formed the Nazi Regime and subsequently built the 'death-camps'? Of course not. Human beings perpetrated that suffering – on other human beings. And even where the great and Immutable Law of Reciprocal Action must 'return' the 'consequence' of a previous and perhaps long-forgotten dark deed upon a people, it is still the human being/s who set reciprocal events in motion to begin with.

That does not at all mean, however, that the "perpetrators of such deeds" possess the "right" to so deliver retribution. That belongs to the Justice of The Light.

"Vengeance is mine, I will repay", states The Law![14]

Therefore, the only sure way to not suffer severe and traumatic "reaping" is to recognise, understand, and live **The Truth** of **The Law**. That process offers the sure mechanism whereby "hard reaping" can be lessened or nullified to begin with, and ultimately expiated completely.

---

[14]Detailed explanations of three key Laws of Creation may be read in the Parent Work: BIBLE "MYSTERIES" EXPLAINED...; and in a stand-alone Booklet: The Spiritual Laws of Creation.

Reader; observe the increasing suffering of the earth's peoples; of those around you, and *understand the processes* that have *brought it about*! The "reaping from the sowing" will surely and inexorably *increase exponentially* anyway, so *learn The Rules* and at least *lessen* some aspects of *"future reaping"*!

0.5   The 'Revelation' and The Holy Grail

As we are presently discussing the life and earthly death of Jesus and how His death, particularly, has created a virtual industry around it, we should examine a singular feature that many writers have connected him to. It is a connection that, for millennia, has imbued many individuals and diverse groups with the unquenchable longing to embark on, ostensibly, the greatest spiritual quest of all – the search for The Holy Grail. The numerous stories that history holds about this worthy task are steeped in the highest and noblest aspirations that human beings could possibly bring to bear on any endeavour.

The key element in the search for The Holy Grail is the seemingly inherent "knowing" that it is an object so holy and sublime that its very existence seems supra-earthly in nature. To seek so assiduously for something so apparently unattainable over such a long period of time carries with it a certain kind of nobleness-of-spirit almost worthy of the object itself. For all that, however, no one researcher has actually produced what can be definitively stated to be The Holy Grail.

It is believed by some to be the cup which Jesus used at the Last Supper, by others the cup which was used to catch His blood. A number of claimants around the world hold different kinds of cups or vessels, but the very fact that there *are* numerous claimants obviously calls into question the authenticity of any to lay claim to possessing *the* actual icon – *in terms of what the object is believed to be and the power it is felt to hold.* This "search", like so many "other-world" research efforts, suffers from the common human condition of only seeing the subject matter from the earthly point of view; solely from the physical/material.

It is therefore puzzling that the many authors who have written about The Holy Grail, even though professing a strong belief that it is something so high and sublime that only the purest of human spirits are permitted to behold it, *can still publish reams of paper trying to conclusively prove that it somehow exists in material form on earth.* Even the many documentary and film makers who have looked at it seem not to be able to leave the material/earth paradigm.

So an object ostensibly worthy of the highest veneration, and which only the purest can serve, in the human mind ultimately comes down to something so mundane as an ordinary, everyday clay or wooden cup – notwithstanding the iconic status of the vessels concerned.

Certain authors and claimants, however, have even tried to link The Holy Grail to an earth-based, Jesus-connection by hypothesising a substitute at the Crucifixion, and a subsequent marriage to Mary Magdalene, thus producing some kind of genus different to the rest of humanity by virtue of a postulated Divine, royal bloodline. And thereby bequeathing to humanity an earthly genealogy carried by certain, mainly European, families living today. That hypothesised "sacred bloodline", at least for them, apparently seems to be, or hold, the secret of The Holy Grail.

How insidiously influential such damagingly-incorrect ideas can become is evident from unprecedented interest in runaway book sales of one publication on exactly this subject. The motion picture about it was a blockbuster, thus further influencing many millions more globally and taking them all away from the actual truth of it – *a Truth crucially vital for all human beings to know.* So now, for increasing numbers it would seem, The Holy Grail was, or perhaps still is, a woman.

Clearly, a woman's body *is* a vessel in living form. It receives, and it delivers. Unfortunately for such believers, however, it is not, or ever was, or ever could be, the pure Vessel, the Pure Chalice, that is the *true* Holy Grail!

In any case, who dares ask the obvious question: "Where are the pure human spirits *down here* who would be worthy enough to hold or guard it?" None! Why? Quite simply:

Because the true and <u>only</u> Holy Grail is <u>not</u> of the earth!

How could it possibly be? That is *why* it <u>is</u> so Holy! We, therefore, cannot ever actually see it in its "living reality" – let alone get anywhere near it.

The **form** that is associated with The Holy Grail – that of a Chalice – is known simply by virtue of the fact that especially blessed ones long ago received a "radiated picture" of it from out of the Highest Realms of the Eternal Part of Creation. From them, through their writings, it entered the consciousness of a particular group of humanity whose "collective spirit" was thereby awakened to a longing to seek it out. The process should be seen as something akin to a "subconscious seeding" of a vital, indeed crucial, piece of knowledge for global humanity. Even in recent times, others have received "pictures" about it as well.

"Music Forms", a book by Geoffrey Hodson, offers a tantalising glimpse into what Wagner may have seen – or at the very least perceived – when writing his great work, Parsifal. Dr Gordon Kingsley, Music Director of Beverley Hills Church in Hollywood, California, worked with Geoffrey Hodson on this project. Hodson was renowned for his amazing "second-sight" abilities, and employed it to analyse the forms of some of the noted classics from the great composers. Wagner's "Parsifal" was one chosen. Parsifal is the primary figure in the "legend" of The Holy Grail.

In "The Overture From Parsifal", Dr Kingsley offers his comments on what he believes the music represents and symbolises. A few short extracts indicate the sense of majesty he perceived in it. From bars 45-47, p. 32-33:

0.5.1   The Eucharistic Motif

> "In his music drama "Parsifal" Richard Wagner reached a height of sublimity which even he had not previously attained ... there is added another element – sacredness.
>
> We are on holy ground. The first sounds of the prelude convey a sanctity not of this world, a peace, indeed, which passeth all understanding. It is the motive of the Eucharist. - - - '...it is the old, old story of man's ascent to God. It is only natural that the composer should represent this conception in a musical motive which in itself seeks to carry the listener to higher realms'."

0.5.2 The Grail Motif

> "The Grail is the chalice which contained the 'life-blood' whose ruby radiance streaming forth in blessing, enveloped everything within the sphere of its mighty influence. The very structure of the music suggests this all-embracing benediction..."

Geoffrey Hodson described what he observed in each of the two Motif compositions. More importantly in this case, he also produced colour-prints of what he *saw*; a Chalice clearly not of the earth. As with the other great compositions chosen for the project, the pictures really are "worth a thousand words". For Kingsley and Hodson to, respectively, bring forth such sublime words and pictures from the great work, Parsifal, Wagner must surely have perceived that the Grail Chalice – **The Holy Grail** – *was* supra-earthly in nature.

That being the case, why the continual attempts by so many Grail researchers, historically, to tie it to Jesus on earth? For once the tidings of it reached all the way down to earth through the few gifted to perceive its existence, the answer *was always available to any earnest seeker dedicated to unearthing the mystery of it.*

Since many researchers *have* connected The Holy Grail with Jesus and His earthly Mission, this is the appropriate point to *reveal what it really is.* Despite the fact that those same researchers have vainly attempted to make it some kind of earthly object imbued with supra-earthly power, *in the strangest paradox* the very nature of their research *clearly indicates something <u>not</u> of the earth*.

A clue lies in the words He spoke to Pilate on the day of their fateful meeting: *"My kingdom is not of this world."* His words clearly indicate something *vastly different* to the ongoing notion of any kind of *earthly* association. The words reveal that in the final analysis *direct* connections to Jesus not only *do not* lie in the earthly, they ultimately *cannot*.

By virtue of its supra-earthly nature, The Holy Grail can truly be stated to be a "Sacred and Holy Vessel". Over centuries and even to this day men have racked their brains to try to solve what is ultimately a Divine Mystery. It is most certainly a mystery in the sense that we can never ever behold it or know anything of it in its living reality. It is not, however, a mystery about **what it is** or, indeed, that it **really does exist**.

From The Bible, the "Revelation of John" tells us what The Holy Grail **actually is**. Dr Kingsley's comments about the "life-blood" streaming forth in blessing are surprisingly insightful.

> Then He said to me, "**It has come! I, the Alpha and the Omega, the beginning and the end. I will freely give to the thirsty from the <u>fountain</u> of the water of life!**"

> (Revelation 19:6 Fenton.
> Emphases mine.)

Through just those few stupendous words we can more readily understand parts of the legend of The Holy Grail where, if the power, "the water of life" that streams forth from The Chalice, is withdrawn, *everything* decays and dies including, of course, *unbelieving humanity*. The *actual* Holy Grail, therefore, is what we are all meant to recognise and know as literally the *"fountain of the water of life"* dispensing Divine Power for all of Creation, and thus for all here on earth too.

From God, through His Will: Imanuel – the Alpha and the Omega!

The Holy Grail is thus the Highest Creation of God!

Grail researchers need only adjust their thinking to this inviolable Truth and very much that is regarded as unknowable would quickly fall into place. Determined but ultimately fruitless efforts to prove some kind of Jesus/Holy Grail/earth-connection deny Him His very Origin from out of The Divine. The Lawful and humanly-unbridgeable gulf naturally existing between such Divine sublimity and our far lower level of earthly humanity automatically precludes, as a matter of course, any such connection.

Jesus came to earth to lead humanity back to **The Light** through the knowledge of **The One Law**. He therefore gifted all on earth the opportunity to return from whence we originally came – our true home in a Higher Realm. [We all surely know His words of Divine Love which reveal that fact: 'In my Father's House are many mansions. I go to prepare a place for you.'] However, any possible 'return home' is absolutely predicated on living that **One Law** *inherent* in His **Divine Essence**; i.e.: **Creation-Law!**

He did not come to found a Divine bloodline; by any standard a *nonsense-notion* focusing *solely* on human ego. Yet the extreme foolishness of such an idea nevertheless continues to be promoted. Men had became so entangled in wrong ideas and teachings that *the way home was effectively lost.* Had The Love of The Almighty not inclined towards an erring and spiritually-sinking humankind to send a Part of Himself to earth in Jesus, mankind would have sunk irretrievably. He was not sent to die, therefore, *but to rescue mankind.*

Despite all the trials and indignities He suffered, He did not shun physical death when it drew near but remained resolute, deliberately facing it for the sake of **The Truth** He brought down into the World of Matter. With His blood on the Cross, He put **His seal of Conviction** on *all* that He had *said* and *lived*. With His death, the way to **The Light** was now open.

He had won the victory for **The Love of The Father**, for the **Love of Truth** and the *Love of Man*. For He had subjugated the Powers and forces that had striven to destroy **His Message and His Work**! And therewith, as the incontrovertible historical record unequivocally reveals, man's *faith* in **The Truth** of **His Word** was *strengthened* by **His Victory**. *So Jesus died* for – thus **because of** – *the sins of men*.

If He had given up His Work and fled from His enemies, doubt would have assailed the faithful. The seeds of Truth He sowed in the spirits and consciousness of men then would not have taken root to subsequently spread to all corners of the earth.

Had it not been for *the sin* of *turning away* from **The Creator and His Perfect Laws** and thus *introducing* dark and evil forms onto the earth in the first place, *Jesus would have been spared His Coming, His suffering and His death on the Cross.*

It is correct, therefore, to say that for the sake of 'the sin' which led to mankind's 'fall', Jesus came, suffered and was crucified, but that irrefutable fact is not a blessing for Christians or mankind in any shape or form. Those who had the chance to save Him from a terrible end – the once-chosen and blessed Jewish race – agitated for Barabbas over The Son of God. To Pilate, they shouted: 'Crucify Him'. Standing as an *indictment* against all of mankind from that singularly-dark moment of far-reaching portent, it was and still is an especially damning indictment against the Jewish race. For even today, they still refuse to recognise that **The One** sent to them *at their petition,* really was their **Awaited One** at that time.

His Crucifixion was not, and could never ever be, an act of "necessary sacrifice" to take away the sins of a weak and spiritually-lazy, earthly humanity. The millions upon millions of Crucifixes that have flooded the earth for millennia should thus be looked upon *far differently* to what has been the case thus far.

> Yes, the Crucifix *should* be approached with awe and reverence, **but see it for what it really is, and therefore what it truly means!**

0.6 Crucifixion of The Son Of God: Medical Forensics Speak

Up to this point we have examined a number of issues of contentious moment centred on the life, death and its aftermath for Jesus, The Son of God. Irrespective of the many differing viewpoints about these events, however, a clear and absolutely unequivocal Truth is nonetheless sacrosanct here. And that is:

That the actual happenings in the Life and death of Jesus could only have occurred according to firmly established, inviolable Laws. As we have already explained, it is impossible for anything to take place except under precise and lawful processes, irrespective of what human/Christian opinion – either from lay persons or academics – might wish to state or believe.

Since that *is* an inviolable Truth in itself, let us put aside all selfish notions of how wonderful it all was that The Son of God Himself was sent down to this earth in an act of selfless Love on the part of The Almighty to save **us** from **our** sins. Instead, and from a scientific/medical perspective, let us *really and closely* examine the whole process of the Crucifixion of Jesus in a probing, 'blow-by-blow', assessment of His 'journey of terrible suffering'.

While doing so, we should very seriously understand that the incredible pain He suffered throughout *never let up*. It was *constant*. It was not at any time relieved by 'first-aid' or convenient pain-killers such as we would immediately grasp for at the onset of even very mild, 'inconvenient', pain.

From childhood, Christians are conditioned with a mindset which *superficially* and ***incomprehensibly*** says that Jesus suffered and died on The Cross to save *them* from **their** sins. Nothing, however, about what that suffering *really meant* **for Him**. Not, however, for the 'believing Christian' who will *never ever* experience such a thing, but who nonetheless preens himself with sickening false piety in the truly strange belief that he is 'absolved' from all **his** sins and 'thereby saved'.

That being the perverse and pervading belief in Christendom, let us all journey with Jesus to His agonising death. Whilst on that grievous walk to His place of execution, we should put aside every shred of 'religious' thought, and – ***objectively*** and ***logically*** – try to fathom *how* and *why* around two billion otherwise well-meaning humans on earth can *accept* and even *strongly promote* a belief whereby the excruciatingly-painful torture that **The Son Of God** was cruelly subjected to can *somehow* be the *'right thing'*. Even in an earthly Court of Law, such an idea would be 'thrown out' as unjust. Yet so many believe that **'The Power of All Creation'** would nonetheless *sanctify* such an *appalling* injustice.
[Perhaps we should **all** have long-understood that just as **The Creator** is **Perfect Love: He** is *also* **Perfect Justice!**]

Firstly, then, we should watch the terrible 'scourging' by Roman soldiers. Secondly; the mocking and the placing of a 'crown of thorns' upon His head. Next; accompany Him every step of His cruelly-agonising 'death-walk' laden under the crushing weight of a heavy wooden beam. And thence finally arrive with Him at Golgotha: His place of execution.

Are there any hand-clapping, 'praise the Lord' Hallelujahs there? No! Of course not. It is too cruel, too painful, *too unbelievable*. Yet every Easter on so-called 'Good Friday', hundreds of millions of Christians in their thousands of Churches across the world perversely 'celebrate' this *worst* of *all* murders.

"BLACK FRIDAY!" That is the reality for all time.

Note: The medical and forensic analyses of the Crucifixion of Jesus we now outline are sourced from the History Channel Documentary: **"Crucifixion"**; screened on **'Black Friday'**, 2009. It is a harrowing Documentary that *all* Christians should view, for it is the most graphic depiction of Jesus's painful suffering to date. [In this writer's view, far more so than Mel Gibson's, "The Passion of The Christ"; itself regarded as a very graphic depiction of The Crucifixion.]

For our elucidation, the primary contributors on the medical forensics associated with the *Biblical/historical narrative* of the **Crucifixion of Jesus** are:

- **Dr. David Ball, M.D.**
  ER Chief, Ret., Tri-Lakes Medical Center.

- **Dr. Robert M. Norris, M.D.**
  ER Chief, Stanford Medical Center.

- **Jonathan Reed, Ph.D.**
  Professor, University of La Verne.

- **Richard J. Hoffman, Ph.D.**
  Professor, San Francisco State University.

- **Sarah Stroud, Ph.D.**
  Professor, University of Washington.

- **Dr. Mark Benecke.**
  Forensic Biologist.

- **Daniel Smith-Christopher, Ph.D.**
  Professor, Loyola Marymount University.

This particular segment of our overall journey of *logical* enlightenment is offered as a help primarily to those Christians who are 'content with their faith'. However, the 'blind-faith' attitude that many Christians seemingly display is really no faith at all, for it simply demands that *the faithful* 'accept without question' all they are told. Specifically and especially on the question of whether or not Jesus came to earth 'to take on the sins of men' and 'die on The Cross to save them'; without keen examination of this subject from either the 'Christian teacher' or the 'Christian follower' to ensure an absolutely correct answer – i.e., according to **The Will Of God Whom** all Christians will state they want to serve – the warning of a very well known key Bible Scripture should be the primary driver to "get it right"!

"When the blind lead the blind, all will fall into the ditch." [abyss]

Since there are a number of quite different interpretations and beliefs around this question, it is patently obvious that many Christian 'flocks' have thus 'not got it right' at all. Yet every one will *swear* they are 'saved' by 'their' belief, or their 'group interpretation'. Unfortunately, as we all surely and logically understand, the *correct answers* that must *inherently reside* in the events and meaning surrounding Jesus's death *cannot possibly* allow for an *infinite number* of 'saviour-scenarios' here.
The knowledgable analyses of the above contributors will help the average or 'seeking' Christian make more sense of a momentous and portentous event that ultimately affects **all** of humankind.

Crucifixion: A slow death of maximum suffering, used as a method of Capital Punishment for over 3,000 years. It was practised in various forms long before Roman Legions occupied the land of Judea at the time of Jesus. From the more simple but excruciatingly-painful practice of 'staking' a body to hang suspended from an upright stake, true crucifixion – the body affixed in the 'crucifix position' on a wooden 'cross' – was perhaps a 'torturous refinement' of 'staking'.

Death by crucifixion was a very effective way to discipline the many peoples conquered by Rome. Her vast Empire required policing methods designed to ensure that the "Pax Romana" – 'The

57

Peace of Rome' – was kept. Crucifying criminals, dissidents and revolutionaries alike who threatened that 'peace' set a severe example to others contemplating the same. Instilling fear of a terrible and agonisingly-painful death in Roman subjects probably did help hold the 'Pax Romana'; for crucified victims were often left to decompose on the cross for all to see. A further unsettling dimension for both the crucified and the travelling public was the fact that crows often sat on the heads of victims to peck at the eyes. Perhaps the most notable crucifixion *event* was the execution of 6,000 gladiators taken from the slave Army of Spartacus after his defeat. They stretched 125 miles along the Appian Way from Capua to Rome.

By the time Jesus walked the earth, the Romans had well-perfected the 'art' of crucifixion as we know it today. Two forms of 'the cross of crucifixion' were used by the Legions. The **Tau** – in the shape of a **Capital T**; and the **Latin** – in the shape of a **lower-case t**. Both consisted of two parts: The **Stipe**, the *upright beam*; and the **Patibulum**, the *cross-member*.

The no-nonsense approach of the Roman Army to all they undertook would have ensured a practical and efficient method for crucifying the countless thousands unfortunate enough to earn that particular death sentence. So the **Tau**, being simpler, was therefore probably more commonly used because the top of the **Stipe** is in the reach of soldiers.

A new look at the whole question of Roman-style crucifixion offers greater insights into the death of Jesus. Notwithstanding the obvious fact that Roman soldiers were well practised in the *mechanics* of crucifixion, considerable effort in time and manpower would nonetheless have been required to nail and/or affix the many tens of thousands crucified over the term of the Roman Empire; if the Latin Cross was the preferred option.

The simpler and thus more likely method was to first set the upright beam – the **Stipe** – in the ground. The wooden cross-member – the *mortised* **Patibulum** weighing about 100 pounds to which the victim was affixed – was then lifted up by soldiers and fitted onto a matching tenon on the **Stipe**.

0.6.1 The Roman 'Flagrum': The 'Scourging' of "The Son Of God"

scourge *n.* **1.** A whip used to inflict punishment.

2. Any means of inflicting severe suffering, vengeance, or punishment

scourging *tr.v.* **1.** to flog.

'Scourging' commonly preceded crucifixion. It was carried out by soldiers wielding the Flagrum, a Roman whip designed to flay skin, tissue and muscle, and thus inflict serious wounds and excruciating pain. It consisted of several strips of leather into which were tied pieces of metal, nails, glass, bone and lead weights; basically anything that would cut into flesh.

According to Richard J. Hoffman:

> "To be crucified was to say that you were no better than a slave. You are worthy of death. And part of the crucifixion process – you might say the drama of crucifixion – was to scourge you."

The victim was stripped of all clothing save perhaps for loin coverings, and tied by the hands to a wooden post. Two Roman soldiers would stand either side of the victim and alternate whip strokes. The severity of the flogging was largely determined by the viciousness of the soldiers. Long-practised in war and killing, soldiers of the super-efficient, well-disciplined and ruthless Roman Army were very far removed from the more squeamish nature of modern Western peoples who often require counselling as a way of coping with what are often just the simple realities of life on earth. Since crucifixion as a punishment was common, soldiers would often experiment on the hapless victims. Dr. David Ball explains:

> "What you would expect from a Roman Flagrum would be complete tearing away of the skin down to the ribs. And this results in bruising to the intercostal muscles, which impairs respiration ... and actually causes bruising to the lungs... And that leads

to a very serious medical problem called 'pulmonary contusion'. That will lead to 'pulmonary oedema' and impaired respiration. It is a very serious injury."

In this medical-trauma analysis of 'scourging' and crucifixion, we reiterate that it is an analysis of *the suffering of Jesus*, primarily as recorded in The Bible.

Dr Ball notes that the wounds inflicted on a human being by scourging with the Roman Flagrum [are] "...so severe that it has been compared to a shotgun blast at close range."
And Robert M. Norris says:

> "The muscles would have been torn, hanging; basically ribbons of flesh that were bleeding profusely ... deep tissues of larger vessels that can't clamp down so easily. Profuse bleeding decreases blood supply leading to hypo-bulimic shock ... not enough blood circulating around heart to profuse vital tissues; the muscles and the organs."

A prime purpose of 'scourging' was to:

> "Create a mutilated body up on the cross ... [for] ... a mutilated, visceral experience on the part of the viewers who were attending the crucifixion. ... We don't really know how Jesus was scourged. The Gospels don't give us much detail. But it's quite possible that it was fairly severe because Jesus dies within a day. And He dies before nightfall."
>
> (Jonathan Reed, Ph.D.)

> "He was beaten nearly to death. He was macerated. He was bruised. He had massive damage to the backside, and massive damage to the inter-costal muscles, and massive damage to the lungs and the kidneys themselves through the bruising process."
>
> (David Ball, M.D.)

Narration: 'When the scourging is finished, Jesus's back is an unrecognisable mass of torn and bleeding tissue. This brutal beating will dramatically affect the final hours of Jesus's life.'

0.6.2 The 'Burden' of the Cross

The present, widely accepted, notion in Christendom is that Jesus was made to carry or drag a complete **Latin Cross** weighing several hundred pounds roughly a mile to Golgotha, then nailed onto it whilst it was on the ground, both raised up together, and the Cross then positioned in a pre-prepared hole. If that *were* the true scenario, it would have taken a superhuman effort to carry or drag such a weight that distance with a body severely-weakened and already near death as a result of the torture and mutilation at the hands of the Roman soldiers ordered to 'scourge' Him. The Bible narrative reports that 'Simon of Cyrene' was seconded to carry Jesus's Cross after His strength finally gave out.

> "I do not think it is either practical – from a Roman perspective – to have individuals carry entire crosses. Nor do I think it is likely possible as a physical feat."
>
> (Sarah Stroud, Ph.D.)

Experts generally agree it is more likely that Jesus would have carried only the Patibulum, which nonetheless weighed around 100 pounds – a huge weight for a badly tortured man to carry any distance.

> "For this point the victim would already be in some degree of shock due to blood loss from the scourging. So now we've put a 100 pound beam on the person's back; strapped their hands to it. And now the heart is tasked to pump even harder and harder to supply the leg muscles to get him to the execution site."
>
> (Robert M. Norris, M.D.)

Whipped up by Caiaphas and key members of The Sanhedrin, the emotional turmoil connected with the trial and sentence of Jesus would surely have wrought tumultuous agitation among those who watched Him walk His last pain-wracked mile – to Golgotha. The Bible tells us that Jesus fell under the weight of the Patibulum. Norris further notes:

> "The full force of His body and that 100 pound weight on the backs of His shoulders would have been centred on His chest. That slammed the heart against His breastbone, the sternum, inside. That could bruise the heart."

"A bruised heart is a very serious injury. The muscle has been damaged, and so it tends to stretch. And as the heart is pumping, that stretch increases and you have a balloon we call an 'aneurysm'. That 'balloon' becomes thin-walled and can rupture."

(David Ball, M.D.)

This type of injury is similar to chest trauma sustained in a car accident when an unrestrained driver impacts onto the steering wheel. Now bearing the added pain and trauma of a bruised heart from His fall, Jesus is forced to continue His grievous walk to his place of execution.

0.7 The 'Murder' at Golgotha

0.7.1 The 'Nailing'

"The bio-mechanics of a crucifixion is quite interesting. It all depends very much on the angle in which you secure the limbs and all the body parts because this will determine how much physical stress will either be on the bones or connective tissue. ... The maximum stress that you can have on the tissue, on the bones, is between 40 and 60 pounds. This may cause the tissue to rip or the bones to break so that the whole system of crucifixion won't work..."

Dr Mark Benecke also found that in tests with arms set at an angle in a crucifixion:

"...*each* hand bears the whole weight of the body, and not *half* the body-weight for each as we might ['logically'] expect. Therefore, an average weight man will tear away from the cross if nailed through the hands."

(Dr. Benecke.)

Dr. Norris explains that if the nails were placed instead into the wrist, i.e., into the small bones of the wrist where there are [dense] fibrous sheaths around these bones:

"...they would have held. The pain, however, would be excruciating because the large median nerve which provides sensation to the forearm and hand passes right through this area of the wrist."

Commenting on the 'pain factor' when the wrists are 'nailed', Dr. Ball states that:

"The median nerve, whether it's lacerated, or whether it's impinged upon as the nail pushes against it ... it's going to be like *burning, severe pain.*"

The Gospels imply that Jesus is nailed through the hand. In the ancient Greek language, in which The Bible was originally written, the word for hand describes both the hand and the wrist. So the bony area described is where most experts believe the Romans drove the nail into Jesus's hand. They would probably not have relied on the nails alone, so also tied the arms to support the weight of the body.

"The ultimate outcome in terms of how long the person survived probably was dependent in some particular way in how the feet were attached."

(Robert M. Norris, M.D.)

The feet were most likely attached in the 'stacked' position – one foot on top of the other as commonly depicted. This position, whilst encouraging a quicker death, produced excruciating pain.

"If you place the soles of the feet flat against the upright, the individual cannot lock their knees. They have to support their weight with the thigh muscles. Or hang completely from the [hand] nails."

(David Ball, M.D.)

This fiendishly torturous position made it far more challenging for the victim to breathe. Scholars of crucifixions generally do not believe that artistic portrayals in paintings and Hollywood movies depicting a wooden block under the feet of Jesus are correct. For why, after such prolonged torture, would the Romans then offer *any* victim even the smallest measure of 'comfort'?

63

"There are a series of nerves that pass through the feet in that area that would cause tremendous stimulation of those sensory nerves and just exquisite pain from that. And every time the victim would try to rise to exhale, that would stimulate those nerves."

(Robert M. Norris, M.D.)

Dr. Ball says:

"A person nailed to the cross is going to be searching for a comfortable position. He may relieve the pain on the medial nerve and lift himself up, but he creates muscle pain. When he drops himself down he relieves the muscles but he finds the pain has recurred in the medial nerve and the shoulders."

In excruciating agony Jesus tries to find relief from the intense pain wracking every part of His body. He strives to breathe freely by pushing up on the spike driven through His feet. In doing so the exposed nerves on His cruelly-flayed back rub on the rough-hewn post.

"Every time He would lift Himself up on the Cross, that would drag these torn shredded tissues of the back across the rough wood of the Cross, reopening the wounds, re-stimulating the nerves in the back causing further bleeding and, again, causing tremendous pain."

(Robert M. Norris, M.D.)

Dr. Ball notes that:

"There is no comfortable position on the Cross. There is no position where He is even relatively pain-free."

Narration: 'Jesus hangs in agony. The end is near. He's beaten, dehydrated, exhausted. He's suffering from external trauma and internal injuries; all life-threatening conditions. But what ultimately kills Jesus? Today, science may have the technology to decode the ancient evidence and discover the exact cause of Jesus's death on the Cross. ... Since His arrest nine hours earlier He's been beaten and abused. His crucified body is wracked with pain as He struggles to breathe. The cruelty is clearly taking its toll. But what is the ultimate cause of Jesus's death?' Dr. Norris states:

"There were so many things that were going on at the same time. Any one of them at a certain point could cause someone's death; the dehydration, the blood loss, just the severe trauma to the muscles."

Medical experts believe that Jesus's physical deterioration begins with exhaustion, for He has not slept for over twenty four hours. Moreover, since His arrest He has had nothing to eat or drink.

0.8   His Final Moments

"The death-process is definitely underway. ... the scourging started the process with the contused lungs, bruising to the muscles, damaged kidneys."
"I don't think that it's fair to say there is one cause of death on the cross. I think it is multi-factorial, and all of these things are taking place in a typical crucifixion."

(David Ball, M.D.)

Narration: 'His blood-loss is made worse by the constant tearing of the wounds on His back as He moves up and down on the Cross in order to breathe deeply. The loss of bodily fluids means He's probably suffering from hypo-bulimic shock; a condition in which the heart is unable to pump adequate blood to the organs, muscles and vital tissues. On top of that, decreased respiratory volume means carbon dioxide is building up in the lungs and reducing oxygen in the blood; a condition known as hypoxia. Ultimately, this could lead to suffocation.'

"He's probably becoming somewhat hypoxic at this point, Again, from the increased work of breathing, and inadequate blood volume circulating around. He is near death."

(Robert M. Norris, M.D.)

Deriving from His fall with the weight of a 100 pound Patibulum on His back, it is very probable that Jesus is suffering from 'blunt chest trauma'. 'The ensuing internal damage could easily include a bruised heart.'

"When an individual has sustained a bruise to his heart, this bruise creates a soft spot in the muscle. Every time the heart pumps, there's pressure on that soft spot that has the tendency to cause a ballooning out. Or, as we call it, an aneurysm."

(David Ball, M.D.)

Narration: 'Jesus's cardiovascular system is under enormous stress. His heart is pumping upwards of 170 beats per minute. An aneurysm puts Him at even greater risk. If left untreated it can rupture. And there's another factor that can contribute to the death of any victim on the cross.' Jonathan Reed notes:

"The pain of crucifixion is unimaginable. ... the pain over time is so excruciating that the bodily functions give out. You die simply of pain."

Narration: 'Any one of these [conditions] can be fatal. But Jesus has not yet given up. According to The Bible He is able to speak despite His weakened condition.'

"He was carrying on conversations that were lucid and clear. So we know that His brain was being adequately supplied at this point with enough [oxygenated] blood."

(David Ball, M.D.)

Narration: 'After several hours, Jesus seems to know that the end has come. The Bible says that he called out His final words – and then dies.'
His final words: **"Father. Into your hands I commit my spirit."**

Dr. Ball states factually that:

"If He had died of hypo-bulimic shock – as some people say – He would have fainted. He would not have been able to holler out with a loud voice and then suddenly die."

Whilst some see asphyxiation as the cause of death, Dr Ball explains why that is very unlikely. He sagely observes that if a crucified man has: "...enough air in his lungs to holler out, he will not be in any danger of dying of asphyxiation. That cannot happen."

Dr. Robert M. Norris further notes:

> "That He had enough strength and enough mental clarity to cry out very effectively means to me that something catastrophic was happening. And He knew that it was happening."

Given the searching medical analysis of the final moments of Jesus's life, experts believe that the most likely cause of death is from His bruised and damaged heart. Dr. Norris explains the process: "Gradually His heart is failing. The fluids would begin to back up in the lungs, around the lungs, and actually around the outside of the heart; inside the heart sac – the pericardium."

The pericardium is a sac of fibrous tissue filled with a water-like fluid that surrounds and protects the heart. Dr. Ball explains:

> "With His pulse rate going to 180 or even more, He is under an enormous cardiovascular stress load."

Dr. Ball opines that under such extreme stress, the bruised heart of Jesus ultimately ruptures. It would feel like a heart attack, and Jesus would know His death is imminent. The ruptured heart continues to beat. With each pulse, however, it pushes blood into the pericardial sac until the heart finally stops.

That is the one, single, blessing for The Son Of God in His whole unbelievable journey of horrific, agonising torture to His execution on the 'death cross' at Golgotha:

For His terrible ordeal at the hands of men is finally over!

> "You've got a heart that is ruptured. It's not functioning any more, it's not pumping. But you've got a pericardial sac that is under pressure. Taut."
>
> (David Ball, M.D.)

The spear of a Roman soldier reveals the proof of Dr. Ball's medical analysis of the actual death of Jesus. Jonathan Reed, Ph.D., quotes the Gospel of John:

> "A Roman soldier takes a spear and sticks it inside Jesus to make sure that He's dead."

The Gospel narrative states that blood and water flow from the wound. Dr. Ball explains what has taken place:

> "What you have to understand is they've gone through this pericardial sac to get to the heart. The pericardial sac is under pressure. The blood has settled. So immediately you've got this flow of blood followed by clear fluid, which is described as water in The Bible."

Narration: 'After about six hours on the Cross, Jesus Christ is dead. It's a relatively short time for crucifixion [by Roman standards], which can last for several excruciating days.
Arrested on the Thursday night of the Passover holiday; by Friday morning soldiers are preparing to nail Him to the Cross. By that afternoon He will be dead.'

The final act played out both on Golgotha and for those in the Sanhedrin who actively plotted to bring about His death, was wrought by a powerful earthquake. Sufficiently strong to shatter the floor of the Temple of Jerusalem, the convulsive transfer of energy from the earth to the great building tore asunder the heavy curtain that protected **The Holy of Holies**.

The odds of *that* particular earth-tremor occurring with such precise convergence to, *ostensibly*, *'coincide'* with the exact moment Jesus died, would surely be in the order of millions to one. That natural event should be *proof enough* of how terribly wrong His execution was, for even the **Forces of Nature** vented their anger and fury at the *murder* of **The Son Of God: He Who** once Commanded *the same* to cease their 'storm-work' activity on the Sea of Galilee with the admonition: **"Peace. Be still!"**

For the Jewish race, what was once the Holiest Treasure on earth – the *sanctuary* of which even **Moses the Law-Giver** *could not enter* on the decades-long journey to the 'promised land' – *was no longer so*. The curtain that formerly 'spiritually-symbolically' protected it, rent in two by the power of the tremor at the murder of **The Son Of God**, signified the *separation* of man from **The Almighty** – *not the opposite*.

It was not a *reconciliation*, as 'Christian academia' will argue. The Jewish Priesthood, once Called to serve and protect that Holy Treasure; by *their* dark deed were made *redundant*. For, shortly after, the Jewish race lost possession of The Holy of Holies and it *disappeared from history*; a *further* indication of the **singular enormity** of that particular crime.

The historical aftermath of the execution of Jesus saw develop among Christians and their Church a radical but nonetheless strange change in perception concerning the 'Latin Cross of Crucifixion'. Initially His death only reinforces the perception of the cross as an horrific tool of oppression. Yet, over time, the *symbolism* of crucifixion underwent an ironic transformation. Very interestingly, the documentary, **Crucifixion**, asks the most pertinent question of all in this regard.

> *"How does this implement of torture and execution become an iconic symbol of hope and salvation despite the fact that it continues on into the 20th and 21st centuries?"*

The answer is brutally logical.

*A Teaching, a Church or a Movement that has **Truth** at its core and as its **practice** would not, indeed **could not**, possibly accord such an instrument of torture the perversely altered state of reverence and even worship that the Latin Cross/Crucifix now holds for around one third of global humanity. Only a **religion** could bring such a thing about, for religions hold very little of **The Pure Truth**. Hence the unbelievable state of hate and violence between religions in the present.*

The path to that detrimental point of 'altered perceptions' probably began when the Roman Emperor Constantine became Christian after 'seeing' a vision in the sky prior to a battle. It is said that an accompanying voice told him: "In this sign you will be victorious." Believed by Christians to be the 'Latin Cross', Constantine's victory on the battlefield thenceforth set 'that' cross as 'the form of salvation' for the Church and its followers. Jonathan Reed notes:

> "It's under Constantine's rule that the cross becomes a positive symbol for the first time. And it's a symbol of Christianity. And because of that, you can no longer use it as a tool for shameful death."

69

So in the strangest of 'turnarounds', the cross, once identified with the most fearful kind of death, and an object to inspire terror in the hearts of men, is now a symbol of piety and faith which Christians now use in the shape of their churches, for their rituals, and in their art.

Christianity becomes the dominant world religion. Despite the long history of cruel torture inherent in the practice, crucifixion is almost exclusively associated with Jesus. Even though documented crucifixions are rare after the Romans, this brutal punishment nonetheless persists throughout the centuries. The crucial event of The Second World War saw Hitler's Nazi regime use this method of torture.

> "It was a display of power. It's always a spectacle, and it's always sadistic. ...it was often used against individuals who actually posed some sort of threat or had committed a wrong against the State. [However] The use of it against individuals who were already victims or already captives and completely powerless seems especially perverse."

> (Sarah Stroud, Ph.D.)

Even today in the Sudan/Darfur region where genocide is rampant, crucifixion is sanctioned as a method of execution. In 2002 Amnesty reported that 88 people, including two children, were sentenced to death by crucifixion. Perversely, then, it would seem; the image of Jesus's agonising death on the Cross remains one of our most powerful icons. Jonathan Reed emphasises the fact that:

> "When Christianity adopts the cross as its key symbol, it also defines itself as a *religion* that focusses itself on suffering, and a *religion* that focusses on atonement. And so the cross itself, maybe more so than any book written, has had a profound impact on how Christians think about their religion, and their religious experience."

Narration: 'Yet the cross and the roots of crucifixion reach back long before Jesus. He was just one of the many [countless] victims of this brutal death sentence. From ancient civilisations to modern regimes, crucifixion carries the same meaning. It's not just about killing. Crucifixion is about torture, fear and control.'

"Crucifixion should be a *warning*. Crucifixion should make us *ask questions* about *unjust* and *horrific treatment* of other people. The cross should be a symbol that says: **Never treat someone like this!**"

(Daniel Smith-Christopher, Ph.D.
All emphases mine.)

The murder of The Son Of God stands as the most heinous crime in the history of the world, for He came to lift humanity out of the depths to which it had *voluntarily* sunk. Human ego and religious power had subverted Spiritual Truth and Law. Proclaimed by the Old Testament Prophets, the subversion of It resulted in a rigid dogma that wrought suffering for many, and meant that Jesus had to come to earth to Light the Way back to **The Truth**.

The later Messengers of His Truth encountered the same blind perversity. The explanations of The Truth which they were called to Teach to the peoples among whom they were incarnated, became – in short order after their deaths – just religions.

Historically, have we human beings ever really revered **Envoys** from **The Light** or, indeed, **Its** Prophets? Almost all suffered from human perversity and mockery, *when* they proclaimed *on earth*. If stripped down to 'bare bones', it is the **adulation of human beings by human beings** that has long-reigned supreme in the world. Today, the rock stars, sports stars, movie stars and the fashion models etc., are the *things* of adulation, even reverence.

That being the case; apart from the regular 'Easter Shopping Guide', what do we invariably see advertised as a *primary enticement* for the 'Easter holiday period' the Christian West celebrates? Yes, there are the Church services. And there are re-enactments of His Crucifixion which, *in no way whatsoever for the 'participants'*, could possibly give *any* degree of understanding of the terrible pain and suffering that The Son Of God had to endure at the hands of blind, religious fools. In truth, it is a *perverse mockery* to re-enact His torturous suffering.[15]

---

[15]It is something akin to the 'annual fast' that overfed Western children in communal 'rah-rah, jolly-jolly' groups take part in for *just* 40 hours to *somehow* gain *understanding* of the plight of children so starved that, for many, *death* is their outcome. Unlike the 'empathists' who receive a hearty meal and congratulations at the end of their 40 hour 'famine ordeal'.

So: On every anniversary of His hideous execution, the one thing that probably most Western Christian children look forward to are chocolate eggs, laid – in the strangest, impossible concept – by a rabbit; the wealth-producing 'Easter Bunny'. Is that surely not the most perverse distortion of a crucial date that all Christians should *fully understand* in its *true* meaning? For in its ***yet-to-be*** rapidly-closing spiritual reciprocity, the long-reaching outworking is one of menacing and *growing* portent for global Christendom.

Of course, it's all just fun for the children, isn't it? That is what Western society has determined as being suitable for Easter. Well, the end-cleansing – ***already upon us and increasing in scope and scale*** – will sweep that and every other kind of appalling distortion aside and away for all time; along with all those who cling to aberrant ideas which distort **The Truth**.

A dangerous aberration stemming from the Crucifixion of Jesus centres on the so-called 'Christian Cross of Salvation'. The *shape* of the Latin Cross produces the *form* of a "sword". As a 'belief-token' or symbol *ostensibly* declaring that by His death on the Cross **The Son of God** took away their sins and that of the world; this terrible and appalling *Christian distortion* of the execution of Christ means that the wrongly-revered Crucifix 'spiritually forms' a **"Sword of Judgement"** for all who wear, revere or display it!

If Christians, particularly, do not believe thus, yet still say they follow the Teachings of Jesus; then how do the two thousand million that make up global Christendom reconcile His warning to the world? In the truly strangest of ironies, He – **A Part of The Godhead** – was perversely accused of *blasphemy* by Caiaphas and others of the ruling Sanhedrin for ***being*** What He ***actually*** Was and Is: **The Son Of God**. Yet He was nonetheless executed.

Since an exponential factor can be readily observed in all events now, let us ***restate*** the answer of Jesus to His Disciples when asked what the end-time would be like. His reply is chilling:

> "...for there shall then be ***wide-spread affliction***, such as has ***not been known*** since the beginning of the world ***until now***, no, nor will ***ever*** be known again. And if those times were ***not*** cut short, ***not a man would be saved***".
>
> (Matthew 24:21-22, Fenton. Emphases mine.)

72

Centuries before Jesus came to earth to admonish humankind to obey **The Law** if they wished to *live and return home*; Isaiah, 'the great Prophet and Servant', had long warned so.

> "The 'Earth' also is defiled under the inhabitants thereof; because they have
> <u>*transgressed*</u> the Laws
> <u>*changed*</u> the decrees
> <u>*broken*</u> the everlasting covenant.
> Therefore has the curse devoured the 'Earth', and those that dwell therein *are desolate*: therefore the inhabitants of the 'Earth' are *burned*[16] and *few men left*."

> (Isaiah 24:5-6, Fenton.
> Emphases mine.)

Now you, Christian believer, and perhaps even you, "Bible scholar"; but certainly all who live tremulously in piety in the belief that The Son of God, sent down to earth by The Creator of all that is good to bring The Living Word to a base and evil humanity – now that you *better-understand* the *true* horror and suffering of He Whom you profess to follow; where in His admonition or that of the great Prophet, Isaiah, do you find the sure salvation of two billion Christians. It is *arrant nonsense*; and *a dangerous death-delusion.*

Do you honestly believe that The Son of God went willingly to an horrific death to save *you* from *your* personal sins? Do you really believe that the Perfect Justice of God is displayed there; that an innocent man should be put to death for *the wrongdoing and evil of others*?

---

[16]The term, 'burned' – describing a recurring theme of End-time destruction that numerous Bible 'scholars' have puzzled over for many centuries – *in this case* does not refer to fire in the ordinary sense. The Scripture pointedly states that only the 'inhabitants' of the earth are 'burned', *not* the earth itself. A full and detailed explanation can be read in Chapter 12: **The Two Sons Of God**: Sub; **Destruction by "Fire"**, of the Parent Work, and in a Sister Booklet of the same title.

Such an injustice is not even accepted in earthly courts of law. If it were, imagine the outcry – from all of you especially. So why and how can human beings who proudly call themselves Christians [i.e., *followers of, and believers in, Christ*] accept a notion that such a thing would be acceptable to **The Creator Himself: He Who is Perfect Love — but also Perfect Justice?**

If you *truly believe* that such an *aberrant* tenet would be acceptable to **The Almighty**, then you must logically accept the notion that the Roman soldiers who *actually* carried out His Crucifixion *were also blessed,* and would *follow Jesus into Paradise upon their death.* And what about Judas? Why has sainthood not been conferred upon him? Surely he, too, must be included among the especially blessed – even *before* that particular group of Roman soldiers – *for is he not the key player in this ridiculous and infantile scenario?*

> If the death of Jesus was a necessary sacrifice blessed by God, then that is the *only* logical conclusion for you to draw. For if you do *not* believe that either Judas or the soldiers *were* so blessed in that way, **then your whole absurd Christian ethos centred round "His necessary sacrifice" fails utterly.**

Notwithstanding the pure truth of that statement, if you yet *still seriously believe such a thing,* **then do not hide behind 2,000 years of earth-time to shield you from *that* most insidiously-evil event.** Instead, have the inner courage to put yourselves in the place of the small group of executioners at His Crucifixion and *actively take part* in the murder of The One Whom you profess to believe in. Be part of that Roman squad on that terrible day that you nauseously commemorate so wrongly: **Black Friday.**

Help to lay the cruelly-tortured and bleeding body of **The Son of God** on that rough and splintered "cross of death". Feel **His** blood spattering on *your* skin – for there are no niceties such as rubber gloves to protect *your delicate hands.* Next, take up the hammer. And with it, drive the nails through **His hands** into the wood of the crossbeam. Ensure, however, that you do it *correctly* so that the weight of **His** especial body will not tear **His *once-**

healing hands away from those terrible spikes when that dark, death-cross is raised.

But as you 'drive those nails home', look into His dying, pain-wracked eyes and say to Him:

> *"I nail you to this cross because in my deed I prove my great Christian love for you because you came to die for me and my sins. Even though you have already suffered so much, I offer you yet more pain and torture. I know you will understand and will one day welcome me into your Kingdom because I have now proved my faith to you by helping you to die on this cross."*

How foolish a belief. How utterly absurd.

Such a belief is tantamount to idolatry of the worst kind, but self-idolatry of human beings and not of reverence and worship of **The Most High** or of He Who was and is a Part out of **Him**.

JESUS: The **SON OF GOD**; designated as both **The Word of God**, and **The Love of God**; that is who you symbolically murder each time you tremulously "...thank him for dying for your sins".

Even the words of **The Bible** – that *exalted* Work which you hold up to the world as **The Living Word Of God** – condemns that terrible act in no uncertain terms. Peter, the Apostle designated by Jesus as "the rock" upon which His Teachings could be built, "tells it like it is". After receiving "Power from On High" at Pentecost and speaking in the various dialects of the region, the Apostles were accused of being drunk by the crowd that had gathered there. Peter countered with the following:

> "Men of Israel! Listen to these statements: Jesus the Nazarene, a Man pointed out as from God by powers, and wonders, and signs, which God did through Him amongst you, as you yourselves know; *having betrayed*, you *murdered Him by crucifixion* through *lawless hands*..."

What happened next? The words are certainly clear enough; *betrayed, murdered,* through *lawless* hands! Was there great cheering that they were *saved* by His "death on the Cross"? That is certainly the *seemingly* unbreakable belief amongst latter-day Christians.

Yet, what do we later read as "The Effect of the Discourse" of Peter?

> Now on hearing it, they were **stung to the heart**,
> and said to Peter and the rest of the apostles,
> "Men, brothers, **what shall we do**?"
> But Peter said to them: "**Change your minds...**"

> (Acts 2:22-23, and 2:37, Fenton.
> All emphases mine.)

Quite clearly, if they *had* been pleased and *at peace* with 'the Crucifixion', they would *not* have replied in that way. The **recognition** for *at least some* there had finally **hit home**, for they were "*...stung to the heart...*", did not know what to do, and were now *afraid*.

As it once did to that fearful crowd then: When the horrific realisation finally dawns on latter-day Christendom that such beliefs are so *illogical and wrong* that they border on a kind of *religious insanity*, it will be among you Christians, primarily, that a very large measure of the "great wailing and gnashing of teeth" will occur. What will you say or do then?

In conclusion: Let us, *in quiet contemplation*, seriously think upon a singularly-poignant "poem" about the life of *this* Son, **Jesus**; perhaps the greatest radical to have ever set physical foot on earth.

As we unequivocally state, however, **will not do so again**, for **He** is **The One** Who *returned* to **The Father**. Yet Whose very Words – from out of **Divinity Itself** – many were "called" to disseminate amongst the world's people. Illustrated in the following poem is an unknown author's salute and great love for Jesus and His Highest and most Noble form of **Radicalism**:
Perfect Love!

76

Radically noble in the sense that He was *prepared to accept death on the cross* – if that was the only way by which He could anchor the Truth of His Teaching in the consciousness of humankind for all time.

Jesus – The Word and Love Of God and surely the most innocent of all – even though suffering the grossest indignities until finally succumbing to the brutal act of murder perpetrated against Him, *yet still offered up the greatest prayer of intercession ever for the senseless blind who committed that atrocity.*

His noble prayer thus stands as an indictment against those who murdered Him then, *and against those today* who still very wrongly believe that His painful and brutal death on *that* Cross could somehow be sanctified and Divinely Blessed by **An Almighty God** as some kind of loving act of propitiatory sacrifice to cleanse the evil and sin of an *undeserving* humanity.

The very words of the prayer itself stand in rightful accusation against such an evil distortion of the great and incomprehensible Love of The Creator.

"Father forgive them, for they know not what they do!"

Thus, *they did the wrong thing.*

Through an anonymous yet spiritually-insightful poet, the pure and ennobled form of the Christ's Mission rings down through the centuries and is **baptised in its own unequivocal message of sublime radiance and great Spiritual Power!**

0.9 One Solitary Life

Here is a man
who was born of Jewish parents
the child of a peasant woman...
He never wrote a book.
He never held an office.
He never owned a home.
He never had a family.
He never went to college.
He never put foot
inside a big city.
He never travelled two hundred
miles from the place
where He was born.

He never did one of the things
that usually accompany greatness.
He had no credentials but Himself...
While still a young man
the tide of popular opinion
turned against Him.
His friends ran away.
One of them denied Him...
He was nailed to a cross
between two thieves.

His executioners gambled for
the only piece of property
he had on earth... His coat.
When He was dead
He was taken down;
and laid in a borrowed grave
through the pity of a friend.

Nineteen wide centuries
have come and gone
and He is the centrepiece
of the human race and the leader of
the column of progress.
I am far within the mark
when I say that all the armies

that ever marched,
and all the navies
that were ever built...
have not affected the life of man
upon earth as powerfully as has that:

One Solitary Life!

Bibliography

1. Particular and key knowledge sourced from: *"In the Light of Truth" The Grail Message by Abd-ru-shin.* 3 vol. Edition. Published by Stiftung Gralsbotschaft, Stuttgart, Germany.

2. *The Holy Bible in Modern English*, Ferrar Fenton, Destiny Publishers, Massachusetts U.S.A. 1966 Edition.

3. *Bible "Mysteries" Explained: Understanding "Global Societal Collapse" from The "SCIENCE" in The Bible; What every Scientist, Bible Scholar and Ordinary Man needs to Know!*, Charles S Brown. Crystal Publishing. Revised Second Edition, 2009, New Zealand

4. *The Holy Bible, Authorised (King James) Version*, Eyre and Spottiswoode (Publishers) Ltd., Great Britain.

5. *The Jerusalem Bible, Reader's Edition*, First published 1968, Darton, Longman and Todd Ltd., London.

6. *Great Illustrated Dictionary Vol's I & II*, Readers Digest, First Edition, 1984, USA.

7. *Music Forms*, Geoffrey Hodson, The Theosophical Publishing House, Adyar, 1976.

8. *Crucifixion* Documentary: History Channel. Screened April, 2009.

0.10   The Parent Book:

<u>Formerly</u>:

"The Gathering Apocalypse and World Judgement; What It Brings – Even Now – And Why" [See Back Cover.]

Available in **New Zealand** at:
http://www.publishme.co.nz

Or at www.crystalbooks.org

Now:

BIBLE "MYSTERIES" EXPLAINED
[Revised Second Edition]
Understanding "Global Societal Collapse" from The "Science" in The Bible;
What Every Scientist, Bible Scholar and Ordinary Man Needs to Know!

> The **Revised Second Edition** of this book is more comprehensive in that it now explains How and Why the 2008 global economic collapse occurred, but also when the seeds that wrought the How and Why were sown, and by whom. [Chapter 3: **The Spiritual Laws: The Necessary Knowledge**
> 3.3.3 "Ten Men Will Take Counsel And It Will Come To Nought."
> 3.3.4 The Interlinked Global Monetary System "Reaping The Whirlwind." A Brief History Lesson.]

> Additional information about the events surrounding the last day of Jesus's life, from His arrest in the Garden of Gethsemane to His murder at Golgotha, is now included.
> The interesting question of the "Seven Churches in Asia-Minor" from The Book Of Revelation is examined more critically. Necessarily using the discoveries and mathematics of present-day cosmology, the revealing conclusion of the true meaning perfectly resonates with the intuitive perception of the great

mathematician, astronomer, theologian and scientist, Sir Isaac Newton.

This book, the result of many years of inner seeking and empirical research, offers *serious* seekers of the Truth a comprehensive understanding of the origin, meaning and purpose of human life; material and spiritual.

Beginning with **The Crucial Imperatives: Nine key points** that *must* be taken into consideration if logical and reasoned answers to humankind's Whence, Whither and Why is *ever* to be understood; the book takes the reader step by step through an understanding of man's **Spiritual Origins, The Spiritual Laws of Creation**, the difference between **The First Death** and **The Second Death**; **Elemental Lore** [of Nature]; **Jesus! His Birth, Death and Resurrection** [a revisionist analysis]; before examining the truly 'mind-expanding' meaning of **"The 7 Churches in Asia"** from **The Book of Revelation.**

The key knowledge helps explain *why* there actually are **Two Sons of God**– final Chapter. It is key precisely because all other knowledge stems from that reality.

On reading the Work, the genuine seeker will clearly see that a conditioning process, set in place by religious authorities from the outset, over millennia has wrought appalling suffering through their inexcusable distortions of the Teachings of **The Truth** that once issued pristine and sublime from the Pure Holiness of its Bringer: **Jesus, The Son Of God!**

Now, because of those distortions, humankind is as a rudderless wreck on an increasingly stormy sea. Our many and increasing problems were not brought upon us by any kind of arbitrary randomness, but through *our constant and stubborn refusal to live according to the very Laws of Life which **alone** guarantee knowledge, peace and harmony.*

At the same time, however, – and precisely through the knowledge of those Laws – the way is shown in *how* we can *change* global societies *for the bet-*

ter. Quite logically, if we continue down our present path for much longer *without such change*, the immutable outworking of **The Law** *will simply bring to an end* all that which *human thought and endeavour* had sought to establish and/or erect *in place of* the immutable and inviolable aegis of: **The One Law!**

CREATION-LAW!

The Parent Work explains the How, the What and the Why!

Available in:

N.Z.:http://www.publishme.co.nz

Or – **http://www.crystalbooks.org**

Table of Contents

4 Elemental Lore Of Nature

5 JESUS: His Birth, Death and Resurrection

5.1 Introduction

5.2 JESUS: His Birth, Death and Resurrection

5.3 "Virgin" Birth and "Immaculate" Conception

5.4 Mission of the "Three Wise Men"

5.5 Resurrection and Ascension

5.6 Jewish Condemnation of The Son of God

5.7 The 'Revelation' and The Holy Grail

    5.7.1 The Eucharistic Motif

    5.7.2 The Grail Motif

5.8 Crucifixion of the Son of God:
Medical Forensics Speak

    5.8.1 The Roman 'Flagrum':
The 'Scourging' of "The Son Of God"

    5.8.2 The 'Burden' of the Cross

    5.9 The 'Murder' at Golgotha

    5.9.1 The 'Nailing'

    5.9.2 His Final Moments

5.10 One Solitary Life

6 Stigmata

6.1 The Turin Shroud

6.2 Stigmatics

6.3 The Third Fatima Prophecy

6.4 Christendom's Bondage to 'Distortions' of Bible Truths

7 Right Bible/Wrong Bible

7.1 The Number 666 of The Revelation

7.2 Fenton's Crucial Insight to The Book of Genesis

7.3 Intellectual Volition versus Spiritual Volition

7.3.1 Intellectual Volition

7.3.2 Spiritual Volition

7.4 Summary of Key Points of the 'Creation' Process

7.5 Fentons Translation of The Bible

8 The Emergence of Language

THE BOOKLET SERIES

*　　　*　　　*　　　*　　　*

THE TWO SONS OF GOD

The Son of Man and The Son of God
What The Bible Really Says

*　　　*　　　*　　　*　　　*

JESUS!:
His Birth, Death and
Resurrection

A Revisionist Analysis of the "Sacrosanct"
Christian Viewpoint

*　　　*　　　*　　　*　　　*

THE SPIRITUAL LAWS OF
CREATION
The Crucial Knowledge for Humankind

*　　　*　　　*　　　*　　　*

WHITHER COMETH HUMANKIND?

The Origins of Man *Genesis and Science Agree*

*　　　*　　　*　　　*　　　*

THE "7 CHURCHES" Of THE
"REVELATION"

What the "Hubble" Will Never See
Sir Isaac Newton's "Plan of The World"

*　　　*　　　*　　　*　　　*

www.ingramcontent.com/pod-product-compliance
Lightning Source LLC
Chambersburg PA
CBHW071830020426
42331CB00007B/1674